P9-APO-387

Trade Preferences for Less-Developed Countries

PRAEGER SPECIAL STUDIES IN
INTERNATIONAL ECONOMICS AND DEVELOPMENT

Trade Preferences for Less-Developed Countries

AN ANALYSIS OF UNITED STATES POLICY

Sidney Weintraub

Foreword by Isaiah Frank

FREDERICK A. PRAEGER, Publishers
New York · Washington · London

The purpose of the Praeger Special Studies is to make specialized research monographs in U.S. and international economics and politics
available to the academic, business, and government communities. For
further information, write to the Special Projects Division, Frederick
A. Praeger, Publishers, 111 Fourth Avenue, New York, N.Y. 10003.

FREDERICK A. PRAEGER, PUBLISHERS
111 Fourth Avenue, New York, N.Y. 10003, U.S.A.
77-79 Charlotte Street, London W.1, England

Published in the United States of America in 1967
by Frederick A. Praeger, Inc., Publishers

© 1966 by Sidney Weintraub

Library of Congress Catalog Card Number: 67-16662

Printed in the United States of America

FOREWORD

Preferences have become the major policy issue
in commercial relations between rich and poor
countries.

Ever since 1963, when the main preparatory
meetings were held for the United Nations Conference on Trade and Development (UNCTAD), the subject
of preferences has been in the forefront of the
debate as to how foreign trade can be made a more
effective instrument of development.

The time-honored principle of nondiscrimination or most-favored-nation treatment in international trade has come under heavy attack by the
poor countries. Preferential treatment for their
exports of manufactured products to the advanced
countries is urged as a matter of simple justice--
that unequals should not be treated as equals. But
the discussions at UNCTAD and thereafter have demonstrated that the issues underlying the preference controversy are indeed far from simple.

Anyone wishing to be enlightened on the subject of preferences could hardly do better than
to read Sidney Weintraub's book. With commendable
clarity, the author lays out the history and back-
ground of the current debate and provides a careful, nondoctrinaire analysis of the economic and
political issues involved in the principal variants
of the preference proposal.

What struck me with particular force is the
way Dr. Weintraub draws upon his own practical experience as a State Department official in evaluating the main policy questions. For a number of
years, the author was Chief of the General Commercial Policy Division of the State Department,

v

and during that period he participated in virtually
every major international conference dealing with
preferences. At some of these meetings, he was
both my colleague and adviser. The intelligence
and wisdom he brought to our tasks were valued by
all of us participating in the sessions. It is
indeed fortunate that Dr. Weintraub has been able
to distill out of his experience this valuable contribution to public understanding of what, even to
the professionals, is a most perplexing subject.

        Isaiah Frank
        Clayton Professor of International Economics
        School of Advanced International Studies
        The Johns Hopkins University

Washington, D.C.

PREFACE

For several years now, a key point of contention between rich and poor countries in their trading relations with one another has been the most-
favored-nation principle. The current drive of some
developing, or poor, countries is for trade preferences, particularly for their manufactured goods,
when these are exported to the rich, or developed,
countries. The unconditional most-favored-nation
principle was devised in an effort to work out a
system of equality of treatment for all exporters in
competition with one another. The desire of the
less-developed countries for preferences is based on
the premise that unequal countries should not be
treated equally--and that only through unequal treatment will true equality be achieved.

The issue is complicated. The concept of equality of treatment is not merely economic; it is at
the same time social and profoundly political. The
desire for trade preferences came after most of the
world's poor countries achieved political independence. Those poor countries advocating preferences
now seek a greater degree of economic growth. They
want more trade, not for its own sake, but for its
role as an engine of growth.

Discrimination, in economic as well as social
affairs, touches on sensitive nerves. This is particularly true in the United States. An exporter
who loses a sale because he is discriminated against
in some foreign market may seek redress from his government in the form of retaliation. In the United
States, equality of opportunity is the goal, and
discriminatory treatment as the path to equality
does not strike a responsive chord.

This drive for preferences by the less-developed
countries reached a crescendo at the first United Nations Conference on Trade and Development--UNCTAD,

as it has come to be called--held at Geneva from
March 23 to June 16, 1964. UNCTAD is now a permanent organ of the United Nations, with its own sub-
sidiary structure, so that the preference issue may
be with the world for some time. At UNCTAD-1, the
preference issue was controversial. It is likely to
be just as controversial at UNCTAD-2 which convenes
in February-March, 1968.

This study has grown out of my own participa-
tion in literally hundreds of discussions--official,
informal, international, domestic--on the preference
issue. As I write this, I am not actively engaged
in policy-making in this field. My comments are all
personal and unofficial. This volume has grown out
of a desire to think the preference issue through
once again, which strikes me as necessary. I think
it is necessary for those key elements in American
society to think it through as well, and I hope this
work will make a contribution to that process.

I have sat at meetings with American businessmen. They almost universally have opposed preferences, mostly on visceral grounds. I have sat with
American labor-union leaders, and they generally
hedged. Those hedging in favor, however, often
wanted to couple preferences with rigid import
quotas. What they wanted was a ceiling on the trade
the developing countries could develop, hardly a
boon to poor country industrialization. I have sat
at meetings with economists and heard scores of
opinions for, against, and in-between; and, in almost every instance, the economists rested their
cases on what they believed to be the politics of
the issue.

I have listened to arguments that the United
States was isolated at UNCTAD-1, since everybody but
the United States and one or two other developed
countries, such as Switzerland and Norway, favored
preferences; and that isolation of this type was not
politically tolerable. The truth at UNCTAD-1, as
will be made clear in the study, was much more complicated, since the so-called proponents of prefer-

ences differed widely one from the other. The suggestion was made that to avoid isolation the United
States should have been cynical at UNCTAD-1 and at
least given the appearance of favoring what the poor
countries wanted; or that the United States should
have made proposals designed only to embarrass other
developed countries. Other than the fact that cyni-
cism is rarely good politics, one wonders how this
would help the poor countries.

Surely--and making this point is the purpose of
this preface--the real issue is to help foster the
trade and development of the poor countries. If
political advantage can be gained in the process--
fine. It seems to me that the way to approach the
issue is to examine, uncynically and honestly, the
potential benefits of preferences--and on the other
hand, to examine the possible costs. One-sided arguments serve little real purpose. This study tries
to make this examination in the context of the United States situation.

I believe deeply that the kind of world that
United States foreign policy seems to aim at--a
world of peace, free choice by nations, and an end
to driving poverty--stands no chance of being real-
ized if the relatively few rich countries get richer
and most of the poor and populous countries get relatively poorer. But this does not mean that an assertion that preferences will foster development (or give
the United States lasting political benefit) must be
accepted unless there is a convincing case for the
assertion. There are, of course, other economic development techniques and policies, but for the most
part this study will not discuss them. I intend to
focus on preferences.

Even though everything in this study is my responsibility, in my personal capacity, I have several
major debts which I do wish to acknowledge--to my
government (United States and foreign) colleagues,
with whom I discussed these issues over and over again,
and whose brain power I have exploited; and to The
American University, which stimulated me to put these
thoughts down on paper.

S. W.

Santiago, Chile

CONTENTS

xi

LIST OF TABLES

LIST OF ABBREVIATIONS

CACM   – Central American Common Market

CED   – Committee for Economic Development

CEMA   – Council for Mutual Economic Assistance
              (also known as Comecon)

CIAP   – Inter-American Committee on the Alliance
              for Progress (from its initials in Spanish)

Comecon   – See CEMA

ECA   – Economic Commission for Africa

ECAFE   – Economic Commission for Asia and the Far
              East

ECE   – Economic Commission for Europe

ECLA   – Economic Commission for Latin America

ECOSOC   – Economic and Social Council (of the U.N.)

ECSC   – European Coal and Steel Community (the
              Schuman Plan)

EEC   – European Economic Community (or European
              Common Market)

EFTA   – European Free-Trade Association

EPU   – European Payments Union

GATT   – General Agreement on Tariffs and Trade

IA-ECOSOC   – Inter-American Economic and Social Coun-
              cil (of the OAS)

IBRD   – International Bank for Reconstruction
              and Development (or World Bank)

IDB   – Inter-American Development Bank

IMF   – International Monetary Fund

LAFTA   – Latin American Free-Trade Association

OAS   – Organization of American States

OECD   – Organization for Economic Cooperation
              and Development

OEEC   – Organization for European Economic
              Cooperation

TDB   – Trade and Development Board (of UNCTAD)

U.K.   – United Kingdom

U.N.   – United Nations

UNCTAD   – United Nations Conference on Trade and
              Development

UNGA   – United Nations General Assembly

UNOID   – United Nations Organization for Indus-
              trial Development

Trade Preferences
for Less-Developed
Countries

CHAPTER **1** INTRODUCTION

Trade policy has played an important role in the history of the United States. During the colonial period, British restrictions on the trade of the colonies helped stimulate the revolution. As one historian put it: "This Revolution was made in seaports from Portsmouth, New Hampshire, to Savannah, Georgia."[1] The United States has used tariffs to encourage domestic industrialization. The tariff, and whether it should be "high" or "low," has been a key partisan issue in numerous presidential campaigns, for example, in 1892 and 1912.

MOST-FAVORED-NATION AND RECIPROCITY

Tariff policy in the United States has dealt not only with the "height" of the tariff (the word "height," of course, implies that the tariff is intended to be a barrier or wall), but whether the height should differ depending on the source of the import. In the colonial period, which coincided with the mercantilist period in England, the British effort was to make the import barrier in the United States prohibitive for non-English goods, usually by nontariff devices. In the period after 1776, the new nation faced discrimination in its trade with European countries and their colonies. By "discrimination" is meant trade treatment less favorable than that given some other foreign country or territory. To cite an official State Department document:

> To break down these discriminations, the weapon most readily available was that of commercial arrangements, by treaty, on the basis of bargaining,

1

with reciprocal guarantees for (qualified) most-favored-nation treatment.
The first such agreement entered into
by this country was the commercial
treaty concluded with France in 1778.[2]

This first treaty, and practically all subsequent trade agreements until 1923, contained what is
known as the "conditional" or qualified form of most-
favored-nation treatment. The way this was described
in the instruction sent by the Secretary of State
(then Charles Evans Hughes) to American diplomatic
officers when the conditional most-favored-nation
policy was abandoned was as follows:

In the view heretofore maintained by the
American Government, other governments
to which the United States has pledged
most-favored-nation treatment have not
been entitled to claim the extension to
them of tariff concessions accorded by
the United States to a third country in
return for reciprocal tariff concessions,
unless they offer to accord to the
United States equivalent tariff concessions.[3]

The key words in the foregoing sentence are "unless
they offer to accord to the United States equivalent
tariff concessions."

The unconditional form of most-favored-nation
treatment

is a pledge to grant generally and in
certain specific matters the same and
equal treatment to the citizens and
goods of another State, as has been
granted or may be granted to the citizens and goods of another State which
is on the point of being a most-favored-
nation.[4]

That is, the United States will grant the same treatment to any country with which it has a most-favored-

nation arrangement as it grants to any third country, without seeking specific compensation in return.

One other preliminary point might be made, since the phrase "most-favored-nation" is itself an ambiguous one. What it is intended to mean is that no nation should be given favored treatment over others which are part of the most-favored-nation arrangement.

> The policy of most-favored-nation treat-
> ment is not to establish a most favored
> nation, that is, a nation that is more
> favored than others. On the contrary,
> its function is to maintain equality of
> treatment and to insure to each State
> that it will at all times be treated as
> favorably as the State which is most
> favored. . . . A more truly descriptive
> term would be the "equally-favored-nation
> policy."[5]

The idea of reciprocal trade negotiations, in-volving what the negotiators hoped were equivalent concessions in the trade field, has persisted in United States practice, at least nominally, ever since the first negotiation with France in 1778 even before there was a country called the United States of America. It was this aspect of reciprocity that presumably helped make palatable to the United States Congress the trade agreement program insti-tuted in the 1930's by Secretary of State Cordell Hull in the early days of the administration of Franklin D. Roosevelt. Tariff negotiation remains part of the United States practice. It is still an aspect of the folklore of nations emanating from the mercantilist era that reducing an import duty is a "concession" to a foreign supplier or suppliers and therefore should be compensated for by them by some form of reciprocal "concession."[6]

However, there has been some relaxation in what is meant by "reciprocity" in recent years. It may be desirable to deal with reciprocity briefly, since it is sometimes confused with the most-favored-nation

principle. Reciprocity has been considered to be
the same as equivalence; that is, the United States
was willing to give concessions in the form of lowered tariffs in trade agreements if the other party
(or parties) to the agreement lowered its (or their)
tariffs by an equivalent amount. It always has been
difficult to measure an equivalent concession; United
States negotiators sometimes seem to have been hard
put to find a device to rationalize to the Congress
and the American public that they had received reciprocity or equivalence. The most typical form of
rationalization has been to show that the trade coverage on which the United States received concessions
was about equal to that on which the United States
gave concessions. A qualitative analysis of the
reciprocal tariff reductions was employed in the
rationalization only when the negotiators had to
justify giving concessions on a greater value of
trade than the value on which they received concessions; the effort then seemed to be to demonstrate
that the concession received would result in a greater trade-value increase than the concession granted.

In short, reciprocity always has been a subjective phenomenon, although imprecise objective tests
of the total trade coverage of the reciprocal concessions have been used to assist in making this
subjective judgment. Equivalence, its synonym, was
also subjective and never precisely measured. This
became clear in negotiation after negotiation between more- and less-developed countries. The less-
developed countries did not import enough goods to
be able to "pay" for equivalent concessions for their
exported products in negotiations with developed
countries. United States negotiators, given their
legal authority, presumably sought equivalence when
they negotiated with less-developed countries. That
American negotiators generally settled for less, however, can be seen by the freedom less-developed countries always have had in altering their tariffs for
development purposes.

The latest comprehensive trade legislation of
the United States, the Trade Expansion Act of 1962,
refers to "trade agreements affording mutual trade

benefits,"[7] which may or may not mean reciprocity or
equivalence of trade concessions with each and every
negotiating partner in a multilateral trade agreement.   It presumably does mean reciprocity in any
trade negotiation as a whole.   The legal interpreters
have not really pronounced on this fine point of
global versus country-by-country reciprocity in a
multilateral trade negotiation.

        The Contracting Parties to the General Agreement
on Tariffs and Trade (the GATT) have, however, made a
tentative determination on this point.   Part IV of
the GATT, which was opened for signature on February
8, 1965, now contains as Article XXXVI, Paragraph 8:
"The developed contracting parties do not expect reciprocity for commitments made by them in trade negotiations to reduce or remove tariffs and other barriers
to the trade of less-developed contracting parties."[8]
The United States accepted the new Part IV of the
GATT, and therefore has accepted that it does "not
expect reciprocity" in trade negotiations with less-
developed contracting parties.   It should be kept in
mind that since reciprocity in this context means
equivalence, the foregoing does not mean that the
United States expects nothing in a trade negotiation
with a less-developed contracting party.[9]

        In substance, what has changed is that the formal
requirement of reciprocity or equivalence in United
States trade negotiations with less-developed countries has been relaxed.   Since this equivalence only
rarely was achieved in the past, in any event, and
really was never measurable, the change appears to
be more one of atmospherics--although important in a
psychological sense--rather than of basic substance.

        The most-favored-nation principle is related to
the reciprocity principle, but the two concepts are
nevertheless separable.   It is possible to grant
most-favored-nation treatment without reciprocity.
Indeed, the unconditional form of the most-favored-
nation concept requires no direct reciprocity, but
usually only indirect reciprocity in the form of
most-favored-nation treatment in return for one's
exports.   It is also possible to grant reciprocity

without extending most-favored-nation treatment, as indeed was essentially the practice under the conditional form of most-favored-nation. It is useful to distinguish between the two concepts.

Under present United States tariff negotiating techniques, the two are of course related in the sense that the United States must receive reciprocity from somebody before it can give most-favored-nation treatment to somebody else. The United States must receive reciprocity from other developed countries in a tariff bargain before the developing countries can get the benefits of nonreciprocity.

The two concepts also are intertwined in recent literature because of the demands of less-developed countries. The less-developed countries for some time have argued that a reciprocal or equivalent tariff bargain between a rich and a poor country was not really possible; they therefore sought a non-reciprocity principle. This they now have achieved formally in Part IV of the GATT.

At the same time, the less-developed countries have asked that their exports be given preferential tariff and trade treatment over exports of developed countries when imported by a developed country. This preferential trade treatment would, of course, be a derogation from the most-favored-nation concept for less-developed countries.[10] This is different from a nonreciprocity request, but the following recommendation from the first United Nations Conference on Trade and Development (or UNCTAD as it will be referred to in this study) shows how the two concepts have become mixed one with the other:

> Recommends that the Secretary-General of
> the United Nations make appropriate ar-
> rangements for the establishment as soon
> as possible of a committee of governmental
> representatives drawn from both developed
> and developing countries to consider the
> matter [of preferences from developed to
> less-developed countries] with a view
> to working out the best method of imple-

menting such preferences on the basis
of non-reciprocity from the developing
countries, as well as to discuss further
the differences of principle referred to
above.[11]

What the less-developed countries have been
seeking are two things: nonreciprocity in trade
negotiations, which in principle they now have
achieved; and preferences for their manufactured,
semimanufactured, processed, and semiprocessed goods,
which they have not achieved. It is this second
point, preferential trade treatment for less-
developed countries in export markets, which will be
examined in this study. The focus will be on its implications for the less-developed countries, and for
United States trade policy.

DEROGATIONS FROM MOST-FAVORED-
NATION POLICY

It may be useful to return briefly in this in-
troductory section to some recent history. Since
the middle of the nineteenth century, the leading
European countries have advocated the unconditional
form of the most-favored-nation policy in international trade, except in their trade with their colonies. The United States moved to this policy only
in 1923. The general most-favored-nation principle
became the cornerstone of the GATT and is the very
first paragraph of Article I.[12]

This, of course, does not mean that countries
always have observed the principle. GATT permitted
the continuance of the imperial preference system
among countries part of the former British empire,
preferences among countries once part of the French
union, between the Netherlands and what is now Indonesia, Belgium and what is now the Congo (Leopold-
ville), the United States and the Philippines, and
various others, all of which antedated the GATT.
Their continuance was sanctioned specifically in
GATT Article I, despite strong United States dis-
taste for the imperial preference system. The

Article I GATT rule, therefore, came to be known as
the "no new preference" rule.

The GATT contains other derogations from the
strict general and unconditional most-favored-nation
policy. Article XXIV of the GATT makes an exception,
under certain stated conditions, for customs unions
and free-trade areas, or interim agreements leading
to customs unions or free-trade areas. This is a
major exception. These are "legal" preferences.
Article XXIV is the alleged international basis for
tariff preferences among the countries of the European Economic Community, the European Free-Trade
Association, the Latin American Free-Trade Association, the Central American Common Market, between the
EEC and each of its eighteen associated countries in
Africa, for the Equatorial Customs Union, and others.
The basic thesis of Article XXIV is that free trade,
or substantially free trade, between two or more
countries, even though it discriminates against
other countries, will augment the economic growth of
the member countries sufficiently so that third countries' exports to the member countries will be at
least as great as they would have been under strict
most-favored-nation conditions without the extra economic growth stimulated by free trade.

The Article XXIV thesis is that free trade, at
least among equals, is more conducive of economic
growth of the countries involved than trade hampered
by tariff and other barriers among these countries.
The thesis has from time to time, of course, been extended to call for free trade among all developed
countries.

The GATT also permits waivers to its various
obligations. For example, the legal sanction for
the preferential trade in coal and steel among the
six member countries of the European Coal and Steel
Community was a waiver under Article XXV.[13] The
Australian Government announced on May 19, 1965,
that it was going to seek a waiver from its Article I
obligations in order to institute a system of preferences in favor of less-developed countries.[14]

The United States itself signed an agreement with Canada on January 16, 1965, looking for freer trade in automotive products between the two countries. The agreement calls for reciprocal duty-free treatment on automobiles and original equipment parts for automobiles, which in the case of the United States would not be extended "immediately and unconditionally"[15] to other contracting parties to the GATT. The agreement also provides in its Article V that: "Access to the United States and Canadian markets provided under this Agreement may by agreement be accorded on similar terms to other countries."[16] This seems very much like the conditional most-favored-nation policy formally abandoned by the United States in 1923. The contention of the United States was that while this technically is a derogation from Article I of the GATT, and a waiver from the provisions of Article I therefore was obtained, the nature of the automotive industry in North America is such that third countries will not be adversely affected. This type of sector free trade only among parties to the agreement was what was involved as well in the formation of the European Coal and Steel Community, although the motivations for the two arrangements may have differed, being somewhat more political in the sense of looking toward a united Europe in the case of the Coal and Steel Community.

The United States has departed from the most-favored-nation principle for political purposes in recent years in its trade relations with most Communist countries, including several which are contracting parties to the GATT (Czechoslovakia and Cuba). It has been argued that discretionary authority to the President to grant most-favored-nation treatment to Communist countries in the context of bilateral trade agreements would be a useful bargaining weapon to achieve certain United States economic and political policy objectives vis-à-vis Eastern European Communist countries.[17]

What has been set forth in the foregoing pages is a brief introduction to some of the history and concepts underlying the present state of United States advocacy of the unconditional most-favored-

nation policy. The policy is in a state of flux and
is under serious attack by less-developed countries.
It is a policy already riddled with derogations, but
in each case there is a rationale for the derogations. What will be examined in this study is whether
a good case can be made for further derogations, or
more fundamentally, whether the policy itself should
be altered.

The basic issue in the minds of the poor countries in their efforts for alteration of the present
policy, and to replace it with a system of preferences in their favor, is to use their export trade
as a means of promoting their economic development.
The developing countries have argued, for example,
that preferential tariff treatment for exports would
give encouragement to infant industries in the same
way that import tariff protection can do this.[18]
Can this contention be substantiated?

There are additional related issues. Should
trade preferences be given only for exports from
less-developed to developed countries or is the
scope for preferential trade greater among less-
developed countries themselves? Is Article XXIV of
the GATT (which permits an exception from the most-
favored-nation principle only for regional economic
arrangements with substantially free trade among the
member countries) adequate, or should less-developed
countries be given greater leeway for preferential
sector arrangements? Some discussion of customs
union theory affecting less-developed countries will
be undertaken for this purpose.

OUTLINE OF STUDY

The organization of this study will be, first,
to give a brief historical review of the most-favored-
nation principle in United States trade policy, trying to indicate why particular policies were chosen
and why and how the United States came to its present
policy. Then, after examining the foundations for
the present policy, an analysis will be made of some
concepts used as the basis for seeking trade prefer-

ences. The heart of the study will be to set forth
the desiderata of the less-developed countries with
respect to the most-favored-nation policy, to examine
the implications of these desiderata, and in particular to analyze the considerations the United States
should take into account in maintaining or altering
its present policy against trade preferences. An
effort will be made to examine in some detail what
policy alternatives are open to the United States.

Although it will not be stated at each point,
the study does have a starting bias which undoubtedly will color the analysis: namely, that the United
States in its own political and economic interest,
as well as in the interest of the world's poor,
should do what seems promising to foster the economic
development of the poor countries of the world.

Notes to Chapter 1

1. Samuel Eliot Morison, The Oxford History of
the American People (New York: Oxford University
Press, 1965), p. 194.

2. Memorandum of May 23, 1922, on "Commercial
Policy" from the Office of the Foreign Trade Adviser
of the Department of State to the Secretary of State.

3. Department of State instruction of August
18, 1923, entitled "Proposed inclusion of unconditional most-favored-nation clauses in commercial
treaties," Foreign Relations of the United States,
1923, I, 131.

4. William S. Culbertson, "Most-Favored-Nation
Treatment," Proceedings of the thirty-first annual
meeting of the American Society of International Law
(Washington, D.C., April 29-May 1, 1937), p. 76.

5. Ibid.

6. The same point, that a tariff reduction is called a concession, is made by Harry G. Johnson, "An Economic Theory of Protectionism, Tariff Bargaining, and the Formation of Customs Unions," The Journal of Political Economy, LXXIII, No. 3 (June, 1965), 256-83, in a footnote on p. 257. The article formulates a theory of preference for industrial production to explain why commercial policy is conducted the way it is.

7. Public Law 87-794, 87th Congress, H.R. 11970, October 11, 1962, Section 102.

8. GATT, Basic Instruments and Selected Documents (BISD), Thirteenth Supplement, p. 4. Hereafter, this will be cited as BISD.

9. The normal convention of the GATT is to write the phrase "CONTRACTING PARTIES" in capital letters when it refers to the CONTRACTING PARTIES acting jointly, and in lower case when it refers to particular contracting parties. United States literature frequently uses initial capital letters when it is intended to refer to the Contracting Parties acting jointly.

10. This study will use the terms "less-developed," "underdeveloped," "developing," and "poor countries" synonymously. "Developed" and "rich countries" also will be used synonymously. The word "nonindustrial" generally will refer to less-developed countries, but when used will include such developed countries as Australia, New Zealand, and South Africa, which tend in international forums to insist that they form a separate category. From time to time phrases like the "peripheral world," or the "third world," might sneak in since they are popular with some authorities; they will mean the same as "less-developed." Countries with "centrally planned economies," or "Communist countries," or "socialist countries of Eastern Europe," are phrases which appear frequently in the literature. In the United Nations terminology, they are a category distinct from developed and developing countries, even though Communist countries may fit both categories. When there

is doubt, the study will attempt to make all usages clear by the context in which phrases are employed.

11. United Nations Conference on Trade and Development, Geneva, March 23 to June 16, 1964, Final Act. The cited sentence is from the recommendation of the conference in Annex A.III.5, "Methods of implementing a programme of preferences in favour of developing countries." The words in brackets have been added to make the context clear.

12. "1. With respect to customs duties and charges of any kind imposed on or in connection with importation or exportation or imposed on the international transfer of payments for imports or exports, and with respect to the method of levying such duties and charges, and with respect to all rules and formalities in connection with importation and exportation, and with respect to all matters referred to in paragraphs 2 and 4 of Article III, any advantage, favour, privilege or immunity granted by any contracting party to any product originating in or destined for any other country shall be accorded immediately and unconditionally to the like product originating in or destined for the territories of all other contracting parties." BISD, I, 14.

13. BISD, First Supplement, p. 17 ("Waiver granted in connection with the European Coal and Steel Community," decision of November 10, 1952).

14. The basic Australian position was set forth in a statement by J. McEwen, Deputy Prime Minister and Minister for Trade and Industry in the Australian House of Representatives on May 19, 1965. In this same speech, Minister McEwen set forth Australia's familiar position that it was different from "industrial" countries, and that failure to have this difference formally and explicitly recognized in Part IV of the GATT was the cause of Australia's failure to sign Part IV.

15. The quoted words are from GATT Article I.

16.   Taken from the text of the agreement. See
also April, 1965, document printed for the use of the
House Committee on Ways and Means containing "Material
Prepared by Executive Branch Concerning H.R. 6960,
Automotive Products Trade Act of 1965."

17.   "Report to the President of the Special
Committee on U.S. Trade Relations with East European
Countries and the Soviet Union," April 29, 1965.
This was the so-called Miller Committee, under the
chairmanship of J. Irwin Miller. Since the formation
of the GATT, the United States has normally not engaged in bilateral trade agreements, preferring the
multilateral GATT agreement. However, it may be useful to note that the Miller Committee recommendation
for bilateral trade agreements with Eastern European
countries, with most-favored-nation entry to the
United States market as bait, does fit the negotiating pattern used by the United States from 1778 until
the formation of the GATT.

18.   See for example Towards a New Trade Policy
for Development, a report by the Secretary-General
of UNCTAD (Dr. Raúl Prebisch), New York, 1964. This
is United Nations document E/CONF.46/3. The discussion of preferences is contained throughout the document, but the essential case for preferences is contained on pp. 65-78.

CHAPTER **2** SELECTED HISTORY OF U.S.

TRADE-PREFERENCE POLICY

BASIS FOR EXAMINATION OF U.S. HISTORY

This chapter will take as its starting point the present drive of underdeveloped countries for trade preferences from developed countries. The United States, because of its frank skepticism of the preference ideas suggested, and because of its economic importance, is the primary focus of this drive. The historical review of United States preference policy will be selective; it will concentrate on those aspects which appear most relevant to the current situation.

The purpose of the discussion in this chapter is to introduce a series of ideas now current but also familiar from United States history. The full examination of these ideas from the contemporary viewpoint will be developed in subsequent chapters.

There are important similarities between previous United States policy decisions in the preference field and the present discussions. Indeed, there is a strong aspect of déjà vu to much of the contemporary give-and-take. This is not to say that a decision taken at an earlier stage of United States history--which may have been right or wrong at that stage--must necessarily be the same at the present point in United States history when underlying conditions are profoundly different. However, it would be prudent to examine the bases for earlier decisions since they may well be relevant to the comparable decisions which must be made today.

The issue of trade preferences is not new; indeed, it probably is as old as trade itself. It was

accepted in the mercantilistic period that mother
country-colony trade should be a form of preferential
trade. This was designed to be of advantage to the
mother country, but not necessarily to the disadvantage of the colony.[1] Preferential trade between colonies, or ex-colonies, and the metropole, later became an important issue in United States trade history, symbolized by the "open-door" policy; and it
remains an important issue today, particularly as
regards the Commonwealth preference area and the
preferences under the Yaounde Convention between the
European Economic Community (EEC) and eighteen African associated nations, a majority of which are
former French colonies.[2]

THE CURRENT CONTEXT OF
THE PREFERENCE ISSUE

A series of developments has made the issue of
trade preferences of current importance. Foremost
among these developments was the great effort exerted
by developing countries at the first UNCTAD for preferential treatment from the developed countries. Together with the question of the new institutional
framework to emerge from UNCTAD, a matter which has
been resolved at least for the time being, the trade
preference issue clearly was the most divisive of
the Conference.[3] In addition to the United Nations,
the preference issue has been and is under active
examination in the GATT. The Rome Treaty, and then
subsequently the Yaounde Convention, which gave preferences in the entire six-country EEC area to
eighteen African countries which previously had enjoyed preferences only in the mother country, widened
the area of discrimination against countries not
associated with the EEC. This has been especially
controversial among the excluded less-developed countries, particularly those in Latin America. The recent negotiations between the EEC and Nigeria, which
would involve additional new preferences further discriminating against outside competitors, are more
of these recent developments.

As the one major country which does not grant

extensive preferences to any group of developing
countries,[4] the United States is, so to speak, in
the eye of the storm being generated by developing
countries for systematic new trade preferences. The
United States is also the logical target of the developing country effort because of the close relations the United States enjoys with Latin America,
since Latin America is the one major less-developed
area of the world which enjoys no substantial prefer-
ences--and there suffers discrimination--in any developed country market.

It is, consequently, worth examining how the
United States came to its present policy position,
which is one of opposition to preferences.

CONDITIONAL VERSUS UNCONDITIONAL MOST-FAVORED-NATION CLAUSE

Even in statements of people knowledgeable
about the history of United States trade policy, the
words "traditional" and "historic" keep reappearing
in describing United States adherence to the unconditional most-favored-nation policy.[5] Clearly, the unconditional form of the most-favored-nation policy
has swept the field in United States thinking despite
its relatively recent institution in United States
history. The United States moved from the conditional to the unconditional form of most-favored-nation
treatment only in 1923. Even then it was done in
low key. The opening words of the guidance from Secretary of State Charles Evans Hughes to American diplomatic officers read:

> The Department desires to inform you
> confidentially . . . that the President
> has authorized the Secretary of State
> to negotiate commercial treaties with
> other countries by which the contract-
> ing parties will accord to each other
> unconditional most-favored-nation
> treatment.[6]

The authority for this executive branch action was

Section 317 of the Fordney-McCumber Tariff Act of
1922.[7] What Section 317 did was to permit the President to levy additional import duties on products of
countries which discriminated in their tariffs
against United States products. In carrying out
this principle of equality of treatment intended under Section 317, the executive branch "reached the
confident conclusion that in negotiating a system of
commercial treaties to make effective the policy of
Section 317, the inclusion of the unconditional most-
favored-nation clause is essential."[8] A similar type
of unconditional most-favored-nation clause later was
written by the Congress into the Smoot-Hawley Tariff
Act of 1930 (Section 338) and the Trade Agreements
Act of 1934.[9]

The conditional most-favored-nation policy of
the United States was instituted in 1778 in a treaty
of amity and commerce with France. Conditional, and
not unconditional, was generally considered to be
the "American" form of most-favored-nation treatment
by other countries in the nineteenth century.[10] It
may be useful to quote the relevant paragraphs from
the first United States treaty with France embodying
the conditional form, and that with Germany in 1923,
in which the unconditional form first was used after
the official shift in policy.

The conditional clause in the 1778 treaty with
France reads:

> The most Christian King and the United
> States engage mutually not to grant any
> particular favor to other nations, in re-
> spect of commerce and navigation, which
> shall not immediately become common to the
> other party, who shall enjoy the same favor
> freely if the concession was freely made,
> or on allowing the same compensation if
> the concession was conditional.[11]

The unconditional clause in the 1923 treaty with Germany reads:

> Any advantage of whatsoever kind which

either High Contracting Party may ex-
tend to any article, the growth, produce, or manufacture of any other
foreign country shall simultaneously
and unconditionally, without request
and without compensation, be extended
to the like article, the growth, produce or manufacture of the other High
Contracting Party.[12]

The relevance of this history for the present
purpose of examining the United States attitude toward preferences is that the conditional form of the
most-favored-nation clause really is a euphemism for
selective preferences.[13] In short, from 1778 to
1923, the "traditional" United States policy was one
of preferences, selective as to country and product,
based on bilateral negotiation; and from 1923 to the
present, the "historic" policy has been one of unconditional most-favored-nation treatment. During both
periods of tradition, there were derogations from
the basic policy; there have been as many or more
derogations from the more recent policy as there
were derogations in the nineteenth century from the
policy then.

The policy of selective preferences was abandoned formally in 1923 because it clearly had become
untenable by then. There were both immediate trade
considerations, as well as the changed position of
the United States in the world economy following the
First World War--changes which were certain to be of
a long-term nature--which triggered the actual policy
shift. In point of fact, the de facto policy for
several years prior to the actual shift was to ex-
tend most tariff concessions unconditionally.[14]

The reasons for abandonment of the conditional
form of most-favored-nation policy in 1923 are instructive for the current examination of selective
preferences. What should be kept in mind is that a
selective preference, or a tariff reduction granted
conditionally and therefore not extended generally,
must by its definition discriminate against somebody.
This was true in 1922; it would necessarily be true

today.   This process has both political and economic
costs.   In the memorandum of March 12, 1924, from
his economic adviser to the Secretary of State, which
was cited earlier, the following sentences illustrate
the political point:

> Conditional most-favored-nation treatment
> permits and often results in special con-
> cessions to some instead of equal treat-
> ment for all.   Comparatively speaking, it
> arouses antagonism, promotes discord,
> creates a sense of unfairness and tends
> in general to discourage commerce.

In the letter of December 14, 1922, from William S.
Culbertson, acting chairman of the United States
Tariff Commission, to the Secretary of State, the
same point was made:

> The unconditional form of the most-
> favored-nation clause is the simplest ap-
> plication to commercial intercourse be-
> tween nations of the equality-of-treatment
> principle and tends powerfully to prevent
> discriminations against third countries
> and all the ill-feeling, distrust, retalia-
> tion, and international friction incident
> thereto.[15]

One additional observation stressing the political aspect of the most-favored-nation principle as
the United States approached its policy shift might
be cited from the comprehensive review by the United
States Tariff Commission of Reciprocity and Commercial Treaties:

> An opportunist attitude was natural so
> long as the United States kept aloof
> from foreign complications and was in-
> tent upon avoiding them.   Now, however,
> the situation is completely altered.
> The United States has become committed
> to far-reaching participation in world
> politics.   The American Government can
> no longer shape its commercial negotia-

tions solely with reference to the results of each particular arrangement.
It must consider the world at large and
must shape its commercial policy in conformity with the political and humani-
tarian principles which govern its general attitude in the international
sphere.[16]

Finally, the following picturesque quotation
from Viner in 1924 gives an expert nongovernmental
opinion of the operation of the conditional most-
favored-nation clause:

The most-favored-nation clause in American commercial treaties, as conditionally interpreted and applied by the United
States, has probably been the cause in
the last century of more diplomatic controversy, more variations in construc-
tion, more international ill-feeling,
more conflict between international obligations and municipal law and between
judicial interpretation and executive
practice, more confusion and uncertainty
of operation, than have developed under
all the unconditional most-favored-nation
pledges of all other countries combined.[17]

What had become clear after World War I was
that the United States no longer was a secondary
trading nation in world affairs, but a major one
which would suffer from discrimination against its
products. That it did not suffer severely before
1923 can be ascribed to "the fact that other nations have not applied the logic of our position to
our trade."[18] That is, other nations did not promis-
cuously discriminate against United States products,
more as an act of grace on their part than because
the United States actively sought to prevent discrimination. What the United States belatedly discovered in 1923 was what the major European trading
nations discovered centuries earlier and then rediscovered in 1860, namely, "if a country desires to
obtain the benefit of equality of treatment for its

exporters, it can only do so by giving equality of treatment to other countries."[19]

There also were some proximate causes for the policy shift in 1923. The Department of State's economic adviser noted that "In recent studies of the commercial relations of the United States with France, Spain, Guatemala and Salvador, this Office has been impressed with the inadequacy of such a clause to improve our commercial position."[20] This particular memorandum contains another revealing sentence: "The adoption by the United States of the unconditional most-favored-nation policy would show, moreover, that the general commercial policy of this country is not so ungenerous as Europe has been led by the new tariff act to conceive it to be." The tariff act in question was that of 1922, and in particular the authority under Section 317 for the United States to impose penalty duties on countries discriminating against United States exports. The sentence is revealing in that it implies some fear that Europe was going to cease being quiescent in the face of the United States conditional most-favored-nation policy, and instead actively begin to discriminate more forcefully against imports from the United States.

Even after the unconditional policy was adopted by the executive branch in 1923, earlier conditional treaties continued to plague United States traders. The United States Chamber of Commerce cited a 1932 agreement between Chile and Argentina providing for import duty concessions on certain agricultural, mineral, and other products. Argentina extended the concessions automatically to Italy, France, and Great Britain, in view of its unconditional most-favored-nation treaties with those nations; the concessions were not automatically extended to the United States. The Chamber report notes: "Had our treaty with Argentina been on an unconditional basis, the United States would have been entitled automatically to the same rights granted to Great Britain, France and Italy."[21]

There will be no attempt to review here the

history of the most-favored-nation policy as it
evolved internationally. There are literally hundreds of studies which already do this from one aspect or another.[22] Similarly, this chapter is not
an attempt to review the entire history of the United
States with respect to its use of the most-favored-
nation clause, either conditional or unconditional,
but rather to examine some key aspects of United
States history which are relevant to the current
phase of international discussion.[23] It may therefore be useful to digress briefly from United States
history in order to sketch in one aspect of the contemporary discussion which is directly related to
the 1923 United States shift from a policy of conditional to unconditional most-favored-nation policy.

In their present drive for trade preferences
from developed countries, the developing nations
mostly seek some system under which all countries
which are called "developing" or "less-developed" or
"poor" receive preferences from all countries called
"developed" or "rich." This is a form of generalized
preferences, or what in the international discussion
has come to be known by the mutually contradictory
words "nondiscriminatory preferences." This desire
for generalized or nondiscriminatory preferences is
manifest in a series of statements by less-developed
country spokesmen. Thus, the terms of reference of a
GATT working party in this field was to study "the
granting of preferences on selected products by industrialized countries to less-developed countries
as a whole."[24] In recommendation A.III.5 of the
Final Act of the first UNCTAD, which is the recommendation dealing with preferences, the issue of general
versus selective preferences is not made explicit,
but the discussion in the second committee of the
Conference, which dealt with manufactured goods,
made it clear that generalized preferences were what
most developing countries had in mind.[25] The so-
called Charter of Alta Gracia issued by the Latin
American countries shortly before the first UNCTAD
stated: "The new structure of international trade
shall be based on a generalized, nondiscriminatory
preferential treatment in favour of all developing
countries."[26]

But despite this stated desire for generalized preferences, the less-developed country spokesmen have tended to equivocate in the sense of advocating different margins of preference for less-developed countries at different stages of development. This idea of a gradation of preferences was discussed as a possibility by Raúl Prebisch, the Secretary-General of UNCTAD, in his document issued prior to the Conference.[27] It was the position taken by some of the less-developed of the developing countries at the special committee on preferences which met in New York from May 10 to 27, 1965, pursuant to UNCTAD recommendation A.III.5.[28] In addition, several developed countries, particularly France and Belgium, have advocated selective preferences--preferences which would be selective by giving country, receiving country, and product.

The significance of this distinction between general and selective preferences will be treated in greater depth. What is germane at this point of the discussion, in the context of United States history, is that the selective preference policy is not new, and its abandonment was relatively recent in United States history.[29]

SOMETHING FOR NOTHING

There was a time at the onset of the history of the United States as an independent country when it was less-developed relative to the countries of Europe, and when there were voices advocating that the United States seek trade preferences. The times were different, but it is instructive in examining the molding of the United States character as it relates to the preference issue to note that the new country deliberately eschewed seeking special favors. George Washington's Farewell Address of September 17, 1796, dealt at some length with the preference issue:

> Harmony, liberal intercourse with all nations are recommended by policy, humanity, and interest. But even our commercial

policy should hold an equal and impartial hand, neither seeking nor granting
exclusive favors or preferences; con-
sulting the natural course of things;
diffusing and diversifying by gentle
means the streams of commerce, but
forcing nothing; establishing with powers so disposed, in order to give trade
a stable course, to define the rights
of our merchants, and to enable the
Government to support them, convention-
al rules of intercourse, the best that
present circumstances and mutual opinion
will permit, but temporary and liable
to be from time to time abandoned or
varied as experience and circumstances
shall dictate; constantly keeping in
view that it is folly in one nation to
look for disinterested favors from another; that it must pay with a portion
of its independence for whatever it may
accept under that character; that by
such acceptance it may place itself in
the condition of having given equiva-
lents for nominal favors, and yet of being reproached with ingratitude for not
giving more. There can be no greater
error than to expect or calculate upon
real favors from nation to nation. It
is an illusion which experience must
cure, which a just pride ought to dis-
card.[30]

There undoubtedly remains to this day a strong
visceral reaction among Americans that one does not
get something for nothing. This is reflected in contract law, in which a binding contract requires consideration from both sides, even if the consideration
is only of a token nature. One-way preferences,
without reciprocity, have a ring of "something for
nothing," and consequently American policy-makers
have looked for the gimmick, have looked for what
the payment really is.

The theme stressed by Washington, that a nation

which looks "for disinterested favors from another
. . . must pay with a portion of its independence for
whatever it may accept under that character," recurs
today in high-level American policy speeches. Thus
George Ball, former Under Secretary of State, noted
the following in his major address at the first UNCTAD:

> Moreover, we should conduct our discus-
> sions during the coming weeks in full
> awareness that special trading arrange-
> ments have historically evolved in the
> context of special political relation-
> ships, and that special responsibilities
> in the area of trade are likely to carry
> with them special responsibilities in the
> areas of politics and even of defense.[31]

Ball developed this same theme in at least one
other speech:

> Struggling new nations now enjoying
> positions of preference and discrimin-
> ation in metropolitan markets may find
> it hard to give them up. Yet, most of
> these nations are aware that special
> trading relations are likely to carry
> with them special political, financial
> and economic relations that will impair
> their freedom of choice or action.
> Given the brooding fear of what is loose-
> ly called "neo-colonialism," special ties
> of this kind may be too suggestive of
> "spheres of influence" to be wholly com-
> fortable.[32]

These strictures regarding special relationships, both of George Washington and George Ball, relate in the present context more to selective than
to generalized preferences. Under the latter, ideal-
ly conceived, the special relationship would be between all less-developed to all developed countries
and therefore involve a sort of collective most-
favored-nation treatment for all countries defined
as developing. As noted in a footnote earlier, the
distinction between general and specific preferences,

while important, may not be clear-cut in a practical
sense.

The idea of not expecting something for nothing
probably is an important one in the psychology of
Americans. A trade preference, granted gratis--with
nothing in return except some abstract benefit for
the preference giver over time as the preference receiver gets richer and thus buys more--has all the
makings of something for nothing. Even if not explicitly on the conscious level, developing countries and their spokesmen seem to have sensed this
psychological point. Thus, they have argued that
all that is being advocated is to correct past injus-
tices they have suffered at the hands of the developed
countries. In the Charter of Alta Gracia the Latin
American countries, in seeking steps to "correct the
defects" in the present system, noted that "stress
should be laid on the responsibility of all countries,
especially those that reap most benefit from the
present unfair regime."[33] Prebisch compared the loss
in income of developing countries from 1950 to 1961
from deterioration in their terms of trade with foreign assistance over this same period, noting that
much of the latter was "nullified" by the former.[34]
This is a frequent theme. While Prebisch did not
use the word "exploitation" or "strangulation" on
this occasion to describe this phenomenon, other
spokesmen for developing countries have.

This wariness of giving something for nothing,
while important on the psychological level, should
not be pushed too far on the practical level. Americans are not necessarily averse themselves to being
compensated for what seems past or present unfair
treatment, such as price support programs in agriculture to correct deterioration in the domestic terms
of trade. The United States tax laws, with their
innumerable special benefits to particular groups,
are an indication that the practice and the psychology in this area frequently differ. The concept may
be that there should not be something for nothing for
foreigners--and when there is, like foreign aid, it
is not popular. It should be noted that under the
guise of reciprocity, the United States has itself,

from time to time, looked for something for nothing
in the tariff field in its dealings with others.
This last point is best illustrated by the United
States efforts in the nineteenth century for a cus-
toms union or free-trade arrangement with Latin
America.

The central theme of this portion of the discussion, however, seems worth keeping in mind. In the
trade field, at least, whenever the United States
sought a concession, it stood prepared, at least nominally and for the most part actually, to recipro-
cate with a concession. This is the central message
of the portion of Washington's Farewell Address quoted
above. It was the central idea of the reciprocal
trade agreements program inaugurated in the 1930's.

It is not the purpose of this study to examine
the history of United States industrialization, or
United States tariff history. Alexander Hamilton's
Report on Manufactures, which was presented to the
Congress in 1791, is well known. Morison notes that
while it fell flat initially, "it became an arsenal
of protectionist arguments on both sides of the Atlantic."[35] The subsequent history of United States
protectionism, fortified by the Hamiltonian, Carey,
List, and similar arguments, has been described frequently.[36] The context of American industrialization,
and the growing protectionism of the United States
for most of its history until the 1930's, was not
one of a country seeking "disinterested favors"
(Washington's phrase) from other nations.

The purpose of the conditional most-favored-
nation agreements entered into by the United States
until the 1920's was to bargain on a quid pro quo
basis. The aim of these conditional agreements was
to mitigate the commercial discrimination the United
States faced in shipping and in foreign markets, and
the bait was entry into the United States market.
Hornbeck has noted that "The central feature in our
commercial policy from the first has been reciprocity. . . ."[37] The United States was willing
early in its history to exchange reciprocal preferences with other nations, and then later to exchange

reciprocal tariff concessions on an unconditional
most-favored-nation basis, but in each instance with
each side giving and each side receiving.

This central feature of United States trade
practice has now been modified in the sense that
strict equality of concessions will not necessarily
be sought in negotiations with developing countries,
although something will be requested of them. But
the request of the developing countries for unre-
ciprocated preferences clearly runs against the American historical tradition. This does not mean the
idea is bad, or that it should be rejected because
it is untraditional; but it does give some indication of why the normal instinctive reaction of most
American businessmen, and of many other influential
groups, tends to be negative.[38]

American policy-makers tend also to stress
equality of treatment, along with reciprocity, as a
more or less consistent tenet of United States foreign trade policy. The point is made in a recent
historical study of American commercial policy that
"The use of the conditional most-favored-nation policy was viewed as a means to obtain equality of opportunity."[39] An internal State Department memorandum of 1924 commented that "The traditional policy
of the United States has been, with much consistency,
one of commercial equality and the Open Door."[40] In
the shift from the conditional to the unconditional
form of the most-favored-nation clause (i.e., from
treating trading partners unequally in the search
for equal treatment, to treating them equally in
this same search), the rationale was that the changed
status of the United States as an international power
required the new form to achieve this equality of opportunity. This is made clear in the August 18, 1923,
instruction of the Department of State to American
diplomatic officers[41] and in the study of the United
States Tariff Commission which preceded the policy
shift.[42]

The concept of equality of treatment was one of
the principles set forth by Woodrow Wilson in his
famous fourteen points relating to the conditions

for ending the First World War:

> III.   The removal, so far as possible,
> of all economic barriers and the estab-
> lishment of an equality of trade condi-
> tions among all the nations consenting
> to the peace and associating themselves
> for its maintenance.[43]

THE OPEN-DOOR POLICY

In addition to the concepts of reciprocity and
of most-favored-nation clauses, conditional and unconditional, as they affect equality of treatment,
it may be useful to discuss the relevance of the related concept of the "open door" to the present international dialogue on preferences. The open door
deals primarily with trading and other economic relations between a developed foreign power and a less-
developed country in which the more powerful country
has a sphere of influence. It also bears some relevance to the question of mother country-colony trading relationships. The issue of spheres of influence,
either explicit as was common in the nineteenth century, or potentially implicit which American policy-
makers fear might accompany a system of selective
preferences, is of interest in American thinking.

The United States, notwithstanding the Department of State memorandum cited above which claimed a
"consistency" of American policy on the open door,
has long been schizophrenic about what it really
wanted under the open-door policy, especially when
it faced a specific issue rather than a theoretical
concept. This has been pointed out by many writers.
Viner has noted: "The United States believes in the
'open door'--except in the case of Cuba and some of
the American dependencies."[44]

Williams has defined the open door as "the maintenance within colonial possessions of a tariff system which applies equally as against all nations"
and the closed door as a policy of tariff assimilation or tariff preferences between the mother country

and the dependency.[45]   Based on this definition he
argues that "it can be said that the United States
maintains the closed door in her dependencies as compared with the open door at something like the ratio
of 365:1."[46]   His arithmetic was based on populations
in United States dependencies at the time the book
was written (1929) when the United States had tariff
assimilation with Puerto Rico, Alaska, and Hawaii,
preferential tariffs in the Philippines, the Virgin
Islands, and Guam, and the open door in American
Samoa and the Canal Zone.   It should be noted that
Williams' definition of the open door, which relates
to trading relations between a mother country and a
colony, is different from that of Secretary of State
Hay, which dealt essentially with trading relations
within a country's sphere of influence.   Williams'
arithmetic mixes the two ideas.

This is not the place to trace the history of,
or motives behind, the open-door policy.   It originally meant, as Bailey has stated, "a fair field for
American businessmen in competition with other for-
eigners abroad, particularly in China."[47]   The first
of Hay's open-door notes came on September 6, 1899 [48]
and Bailey comments that the notes did not insist on
the territorial integrity of China, but only that in
its sphere of influence each nation would not inter-
fere with certain foreign interests.

The world has altered and explicit spheres of
influence no longer are fashionable, but there is no
doubt that quasi-spheres of influence in the trading
world remain.   These are in part natural; as colonies
became independent, their trading relations built up
in previous years remained predominantly with the ex-
mother country.   Trade contacts, shipping routes,
personal friendships, mother-country nationals remaining in the newly independent country, and other
factors, do much to explain this phenomenon.   The
trade figures in Table 1 illustrate the continuing
large dependence of many ex-colonies on the ex-mother
country.

TABLE 1

Percentage of Exports and Imports of Selected
Developing Countries Going to and Coming
from Former Mother Country
(1964 data)

	Exports to France	Imports from France
Algeria	77	74
Morocco	43	39
Tunisia	52	44
Ivory Coast	36	61
Senegal	78	58
Gabon	51	60

	Exports to the United Kingdom	Imports from the United Kingdom
Nigeria	38	31
Tanzania	31	33
Kenya	21	31
Uganda	29	34
Sierra Leone	67	43

	Exports to the United States	Imports from the United States
Philippines	47	41

	Exports to Belgium	Imports from Belgium
Congo (Leo.)	50	28

Source: Individual country national statistical
          bulletins. Algeria, AID statistics, Novem-
          ber, 1965.

But there also are some quasi-sphere-of-influence
relationships which seem somewhat less natural. And
in this area, faced with a practical issue, United
States policy is less than clear.

Under the imperial preference system, not only
do many ex-colonies continue to receive preferential
trade treatment in the United Kingdom, but the United
Kingdom in turn enjoys some degree of preference in
the markets of its ex-colonies, many of them less-
developed countries. This, clearly, is not the open-
door policy. A recent study by R. W. Green of the
British Board of Trade indicated that as of 1961
slightly more than one half of United Kingdom exports
to the Commonwealth preference area enjoyed some
measure of tariff preference, the average margins of
preference being about 11 per cent on those imports
actually enjoying the preference, and about $6\frac{1}{2}$ - 7
per cent for total United Kingdom exports to the
preference area.[49]

The Treaty of Rome establishing the EEC also
contains provisions associating certain overseas
territories with the European Common Market in the
form of a free-trade area. (The difference between
a customs union and a free-trade area, in a technical sense, is that there is a common tariff for a
customs union, whereas each country is permitted to
retain its own tariff against nonmembers under a
free-trade area.) Subsequently, under the Yaounde
Convention the free-trade area between the EEC and
its former territories was extended. The Yaounde
Convention is now in force. It represents what the
parties allege are eighteen separate free-trade
areas, one between each of what are now independent
countries in Africa, and the Common Market countries
acting as a unit. Trade preferences within these so-
called free-trade areas run both ways--not only do
the African countries get preferential treatment in
the Common Market, but the six countries of the EEC
also get preferences in the eighteen associated African countries.

If one accepts that these are legitimate free-
trade areas in conformity with Article XXIV of the
GATT--namely, that "the duties and other restrictive
regulations of commerce . . . are eliminated on substantially all the trade between the constituent
territories . . ."--then they become a form of "legal"
preferences. Even in this case, however, it repre-

sents a form of departure from the open door in that
equality of opportunity of developed countries to
compete for markets in less-developed countries is
denied. From the viewpoint of less-developed countries excluded from the arrangement, it is technically relevant whether the discrimination against them is
"legal" under the GATT, but this formal type of legal-
ity certainly means little to them in a practical
sense.

If one does not accept that these are legitimate
free-trade areas in the sense of Article XXIV, then
they are preferences pure and simple. The United
States has hedged on this issue. The United States
clearly supported the formation of the EEC, and
France reportedly made association of its African
territories a necessary condition; and the United
States did not oppose this condition, even though it
clearly disliked it. When the Yaounde Convention
was signed in 1964, the United States again took an
equivocal position even though it disliked the preferences involved, presumably because it did not want
to enter into a sterile international dispute with
the EEC and did not want to hurt the African countries involved.

The United States has not been alone in this
equivocation. "Most of the representatives" of the
group of the GATT which examined this aspect of the
Rome Treaty thought that the EEC-Africa arrangement
"did not conform to Article XXIV, but constituted an
extension of existing preferential systems contrary
to Article I:2 of the General Agreement."[50] The Contracting Parties as a whole theoretically have been
studying these provisions of the Rome Treaty (now
only of historical interest) and the analogous provisions of the Yaounde Convention (which run until
1969) ever since.

The EEC preferential arrangements with its associated African countries obviously cause greater concern than do the Commonwealth preferences because
the former represent something new and growing and
the latter something old and familiar and in a relative sense declining in importance.[51] In the case

of the United States, its two-way preferences with
the Philippines, which were maintained after independence, are being phased out by stages until 1974.

The African colonies that enjoyed preferences
earlier only in the mother country now enjoy preferences by virtue of the Rome Treaty and the Yaounde
Convention in all six EEC countries; and not only
does the former mother country enjoy preferences in
each African country involved, but all six EEC countries do. A major argument against departing from
equality of treatment always has been that preferences must beget new preferences, as outsiders are
hurt. This is proving to be the case for the EEC-
African arrangements. Nigeria, which exports cocoa
and oilseeds and some vegetable oils and a few other
products in competition with some of the African
associates of the EEC, asked the EEC for association
to overcome discrimination. From all indications,
the EEC has agreed, but also insisted on some reverse preferences, presumably on the grounds that if
Nigeria got too much for nothing, the older African
associated countries would insist on the same. In
the case of the EEC-Nigeria agreement, which seems
to involve only a few Nigerian preferences to the
EEC and EEC limitations by means of tariff quotas on
the extent of the free imports it will allow of the
key Nigerian products, GATT Article XXIV would seem
to be less than a fig leaf.

When this Nigerian practical case arises, which
will involve further limitation of the open door in
a country which is not even a former dependency of
any of the countries to which it will be giving preferences, the United States will have another hard decision. The United States will not want to damage
Nigeria, but at the same time it will not want to
see further erosion of an important principle with
possible damage to the trade of the United States
and other third countries.

And just as the EEC-Africa arrangement seems to
have begotten an EEC-Nigerian arrangement, this in
turn may beget an EEC-East Africa (Kenya, Uganda,
and Tanzania) arrangement. There are likely to be

association negotiations between the EEC and the
Maghreb countries (Algeria, Morocco, and Tunisia).
This, again, will raise issues of the open door, and
of what the United States Government should do in
the face of less than equality of opportunity for
United States businessmen in markets of developing
countries.

These issues of mother country-colony or ex-
colony trading relationships are exceedingly difficult for United States policy-makers because of American tradition, mentality, and practical considerations. These quasi-"spheres-of-influence" considerations, as well as broader considerations of seeking
to concert developed country positions on the preference issue as a whole, undoubtedly were behind the
United States proposal at the November 25-26, 1965,
ministerial meeting of the Organization for Economic
Cooperation and Development to study the preference
issue.[52]

One additional recent indication of the delicacy
of these open-door considerations for American policy-
makers might be given. The following is extracted
from the hearings of September 8-10, 1965, of the
subcommittee on Inter-American Economic Relations of
the Joint Economic Committee of the Congress:

> Mr. Solomon [Assistant Secretary of
> State for Economic Affairs]. However,
> we do view with alarm this increasing
> tendency to proliferate EEC preferential
> arrangements with more and more African
> countries.
>   Senator Javits. That is beyond the
> former French countries, is that right?
>   Mr. Solomon. Yes.
> . . . .
>   Mr. Solomon. The course we should
> follow seems to me reasonably clear.
> We should seek ways by which existing
> discriminatory arrangements can be
> phased out or their injurious effects
> neutralized; and we should continue to
> counsel others against the institution

of new preferential arrangements.

It may be, however, that our efforts
in this direction--and we intend to pur-
sue them vigorously--will be unsuccess-
ful. In that event, we may want to reconsider our own historic trade policy
of nondiscrimination. We must retain
sufficient flexibility in our policies
to adjust to the evolution of the world
economy and policies adopted by other
major countries of the world.[53]

Like the previous point dealing with the American tradition of reciprocity, of not giving something for nothing, this additional point of trying
to maintain an open door in underdeveloped countries
should not be pushed too far. The United States has
itself violated the open door, as has been noted,
in dealings with its own dependencies or colonies--
although not really recently. More germane in the
present context, however, is that the United States
has tolerated many recent violations of the open-
door concept, particularly in arrangements between
the European Common Market and various African countries, because political considerations seemed to
override the open-door considerations, in view of
the relatively small trade involved in the African
countries.

The valid point that should be made is that the
open door-concept is a strong one in American thinking, and this fact should be taken fully into account
in examining any preferences by less to more developed
countries. The more important the potential trade
with the less-developed country, the more important
the open-door "principle" is likely to be. But this
particular open-door strain in American thinking is
flexible enough, especially when less-developed countries with minor trade potential are involved, to be
bent in favor of what at the moment may seem to be
more pressing political considerations.

Or, and this is the point which will be discussed next, the United States may prove to be flexible enough to bend its open-door policy by entering

itself into closed-door relationships with less-
developed countries. This, it would seem, is a crucial point to keep in mind. It is presumably this
point that Assistant Secretary of State Solomon had
in mind when he indicated that lack of success in
convincing others to refrain from new preferential
arrangements with less-developed countries may lead
the United States to reconsider its own policy.

UNITED STATES AND LATIN AMERICA

For reasons related to history, sometimes geog-
raphy, perhaps previous colonial relationship, a common cultural heritage, or a combination of these and
other factors, developed countries are willing to
take special pains in helping certain less-developed
nations which they would not be willing to take for
poor countries generally. This is an important
point which will be considered in greater depth in
this study when discussing a possible regional preferential arrangement between the United States and
Latin America as opposed to United States preferences
to less-developed countries as a whole.

The people of France are asked to make special
sacrifices, in terms of paying higher prices for
such primary commodities as peanuts and coffee and
in giving aid, for the benefit of former colonies in
Africa.[54] According to a number of recent studies,
of which that of John Pincus is probably the most
complete, France "is clearly paying far more than
its share by any criterion" of the burden of economic
aid to poor countries.[55] But the French share is
heavily skewed in favor of Africa, and a decrease in
French aid to Africa is not likely to result in an
equivalent increase in French aid to other parts of
the world. Similarly, the United Kingdom favors Commonwealth countries in its aid distribution.

The less-developed continent to which United
States emotional ties are greatest is Latin America.
The Alliance for Progress is a manifestation of this.
The good-neighbor policy of Franklin D. Roosevelt
was a previous similar demonstration. Efforts at

pan-Americanism since the late nineteenth century
are a reflection of this. Congressional appropriations for the Alliance for Progress aid program
normally have easier sailing through the Congress
than similar appropriations for purely economic aid
elsewhere. The congressional hearings cited above
on Latin American Development and Western Hemisphere
Trade are replete with references to possible United
States-Latin American special trade relationships,
and one doesn't find comparable advocacy of such
special trade relationships between the United States
and other underdeveloped continents. In its efforts
to reduce EEC discrimination in the primary product
field resulting from the association arrangements
with African countries, the United States almost in-
variably invokes the damage to Latin America. The
CIAP letter to the presidents of the American republics, signed by a United States representative to
CIAP, referred to possible United States preferences
to Latin America to compensate for the EEC preferences to Africa; similar serious ideas are not advocated between the United States and other parts of
the underdeveloped world.

The illustrations could be expanded at length.
Walter Lippmann has ascribed this closer relationship with Latin America to the fact that Latin America belongs to the same strain of Western civiliza-
tion as does the United States and Europe. He has
written: "It is therefore a mistake, if not worse,
to think of the problems of Latin America as foreign
in the sense that the problems of Cambodia or of
Zambia are foreign."[56]

A number of the aspects of United States-Latin
American historical relationships are highly relevant to the present discussion of trade preferences.

A United States proposal for a pan-American customs union, or free-trade area, was made at the first
inter-American conference in 1889-90. Bemis makes
the point that the motive of the proposal was to give
United States manufacturers an advantage over Europeans in Latin American markets.

> It would have given the United States
> preference over European nations in
> the markets of Latin America, in return
> for free imports of articles many of
> which were already on the free list of
> the United States. The project failed
> before the opposition of the Latin
> American delegates.[57]

The idea seems to have been inspired by the success of the German Zollverein (just as the success of the EEC today has inspired economic integration efforts in less-developed areas), as well as by baser United States motives. Its chief United States proponent apparently was James G. Blaine, when he was Secretary of State.[58] When the issue was tabled and examined at the 1889-90 conference, the report of the majority of the committee dealing with this issue opposed the idea of a customs union, or what it called "unrestricted reciprocity," on the grounds of revenue loss, and also doubt that the United States was prepared to give up its protective tariff for manufactures. The majority of the committee (Brazil, Mexico, Colombia, Nicaragua, Venezuela, and the United States) instead supported "partial reciprocity," i.e., bilateral reduction or elimination of duties among American countries until they were ready for unrestricted reciprocity.[59]

A minority of the committee (Argentina and Chile) proposed complete rejection of the customs union idea. The Argentine delegate, Roque Sáenz Peña, made an impassioned and lengthy speech in which he stressed ideas such as the need for Latin America not to reduce its trade ties with Europe and the loss of sovereignty involved in a customs union. The United States seems not to have insisted on a customs union; more likely the United States never really had a customs union in mind, but rather thought in terms of what today would be called a free-trade area. As summarized by the Mexican delegate: "In the opinion of the majority, a customs union in the sense of a Zollverein was out of the question. A customs union in the sense of free trade was not deemed presently practicable. But the major-

ity recommended negotiation of treaties of reciprocity." The full conference eventually adopted
the report of the majority of the committee by a
vote of 12 to 3.

The United States later did attempt to negotiate specific reciprocity treaties with Latin American countries, and provision for such treaties was
included in the McKinley tariff act of 1890. However, the relevance of the foregoing discussion, and
the reason for setting it down in some detail, is
that the arguments could just as easily be taking
place as this is written as in 1889-90.

Senator Javits, to cite one person, had advocated the idea of a Western hemisphere continental
union, first by supporting a Latin American common
market, "to be followed in due course, as the Latin
American members agree, by a treaty for a Western
Hemisphere Free Trade Area, including the United
States and Canada."[60] Some greater sophistication
has emerged in the intervening years between 1889
and 1967 in the recognition that Latin America could
not really be expected to open its markets immediately to United States manufactured goods, without
any protection, and still compete successfully for
most products. Most persons still would be skepti-
cal today, as the Latin Americans were in 1889, that
the United States is prepared to open its markets
freely for Latin American products. For example, it
is doubtful that the United States would permit unrestricted free entry to such Latin American products
as cotton textiles, petroleum products, and agricultural products such as cotton, meat, fruits, and
vegetables. One also wonders whether either the
United States or Latin America would sacrifice too
much tariff sovereignty today.

Just as Argentina was nervous in 1889 about damaging its trading relations with Europe, so might
Latin Americans be similarly nervous today. In the
period 1959-63, Latin American export value rose by
17.5 per cent; of this, exports to the United States
declined by 3 per cent (reflecting United States-
Cuban trading relations), while exports to Western

Europe rose by 32 per cent, and to the EEC countries by more than 40 per cent.

Further, the consideration that an exporter of goods already on the free list in the partner country has less to benefit from free trade than an exporter of goods which have high tariffs in the partner country remains just as valid today as it was earlier. Most of Latin America's exports to the United States remain in the area of crude materials, where tariff preferences would be ineffective.

EEC preferences to its African associates for such key tropical products as coffee, cocoa, and bananas are made effective by means of preferential tariffs, and in some cases quota arrangements as well. This is one reason why the drive for world-wide duty-free treatment for primary tropical products, which has been in progress for many years in the GATT and was raised again at UNCTAD, is resisted by EEC countries. Were the United States to give preferences to Latin American primary products, to compensate for the EEC discrimination--a policy advocated by CIAP--it would require the imposition by the United States either of quotas and/or tariffs to make the preferences effective. Bemis has noted that the discussion of reciprocity at the Montevideo Conference of 1933 was much like that of the 1889-90 conference.[61] These same issues can still be found throughout the contemporary document <u>Latin American Development and Western Hemisphere Trade</u>.

What is germane in the present context is that this issue, of special United States-Latin American trading relations, has been debated earlier in United States history in terms not too different from those of today. In this sense, it is akin to the other related issues cited earlier, dealing with conditional most-favored-nation (selective preferences) and unconditional most-favored-nation treatment; reciprocity versus unrequited benefits; the open versus the closed door; and the entire field of equality of treatment versus special treatment for some and consequently less favorable treatment for others.

The durability of special trading relations, which clearly is an issue today, was raised by George Washington. The special preferential trading relationship between the United States and Cuba, which existed before Castro, obviously did little to cement political relations between the two countries. There is some doubt that the present type of EEC-Africa closed-door relationship is beneficial either to Europe or Africa in a political sense, or that it is durable. These are all issues for later discussion, but that discussion is anticipated at this point because of its relevance to the present historical discussion.

SOME RECENT ADVOCATED OR ACTUAL
UNITED STATES POLICY SHIFTS

In closing this historical discussion, it may be desirable to cite some recent developments in the trade-preference field which in a sense are historical throwbacks, or perhaps historical constants since they seem to recur.

Despite what was clearly an untenable position for the United States by 1923, namely, the practice of conditional most-favored-nation treatment, there is a school of opinion which believes that the situation has so altered by now that the United States should perhaps revert to a form of conditional most-favored-nation trade. There are several causes for this: the uncertainty of the Kennedy round of trade negotiations in view of what many believe is the desire of the EEC for the maintenance of a substantial common external tariff as the cement that binds the common market together; and the growing exclusion of the United States from markets where the EEC has a form of closed door.

The desire for a return to conditional most-favored-nation practice because of Kennedy round difficulties is typified by the following passage from a 1964 report of the Committee for Economic Development:

> If it should turn out that some major
> trading unit of the free world should
> be unwilling or unable to undertake
> trade liberalization that is substan-
> tially equal to what is generally de-
> sired, the rest of the free world nations
> should consider how they could neverthe-
> less enhance their continued economic
> progress through the benefits of expanded
> trade, not excluding from consideration
> a departure from the unconditional most-
> favored-nation principle, valuable as
> that principle is.[62]

The CED suggestion does not deal with how one
copes with retaliation by countries discriminated
against, or how the United States, which normally
has a trade surplus, might come out of a war of re-
taliatory discrimination. (Although the CED study
did not deal with less-developed countries, it would
be difficult to see why, if the United States were
willing to discriminate against the EEC, and thereby
abandon the most-favored-nation policy, it could not
discriminate in favor of less-developed countries by
giving them preferences.)

The CED is not unique among knowledgeable Americans in calling for a modification of the unconditional most-favored-nation policy by the United
States to cope with our trading relations with other
developed countries, particularly the EEC. Congress-
man Reuss has suggested much the same thing,[63] as
has Randall Hinshaw.[64]

The desire to hit back against closed doors in
less-developed countries which give trade preferences
to developed countries is typified by the suggestions
for a Western hemisphere free-trade area, of the type
suggested by Senator Javits, or of a variety suggested
by William Clayton. Clayton, a former Under Secretary
of State for Economic Affairs, suggested moving to a
Western hemisphere free-trade area in steps: first,
free trade in raw materials originating in the Western
hemisphere by reducing trade barriers in ten annual
steps of 10 per cent each; then, annual 10 per cent

intra-Latin American tariff reductions on all products;
and at the end of ten years, the Western hemisphere
countries would again meet to discuss what goes after
that.[65] The proposal has a good deal of merit if one
wishes to encourage a Latin American common market,
since it gives some incentive for this by providing
better Latin American access to the United States
market for raw materials (petroleum and cotton and
meat, et al., one assumes). But it should be kept
in mind that this is free trade which discriminates
against nonparticipants. It is not a full-fledged
free-trade area (except for Latin America) in the
sense of GATT Article XXIV since the Western hemisphere free trade would not cover substantially all
trade (it is only for raw materials), and because
there is no plan and schedule for the period after
ten years. But, by the same token, the Yaounde Convention has no plan and schedule for the period after the five years of the convention; and neither
the Yaounde Convention nor particularly the EEC-
Nigeria agreement can be said to cover substantially
all the trade among the parties.

What the Clayton and similar proposals ignore
is that by being conditional free trade--by excluding some countries--some less-developed countries,
as well as developed ones, will be discriminated
against. For a country with the worldwide interests of the United States, this is a factor which
must be considered, even if it is eventually decided
to accept this type of conditional free trade.

The United States-Canada automotive products
trade act of 1965, which provides for reciprocal
duty-free treatment on automobiles and original
parts, is a conditional most-favored-nation type of
response to a problem which existed between the two
countries. Whether or not it will trigger comparable conditional responses for particular sectors of
European industry, which would exclude the United
States from their benefits just as the United States-
Canada agreement excludes Europeans, remains to be
seen.

These recent advocacies of, and actual departures

from, the strict letter of the unconditional most-favored-nation principle in United States trade policy are cited to illustrate that United States policy obviously is not set in cement, but can and does change.

Notes to Chapter 2

1. See, for example, George Louis Beer, The Old Colonial System, 1660-1754 (New York: The Macmillan Company, 1912). Beer notes that under the English tariff of 1660 "the import duties were so adjusted as to give many colonial products marked advantages over those of foreign nations. The tariff of 1660 rated English Colonial ginger, indigo, cotton, sugar, and tobacco much lower than the foreign competing products." (I, 133)

2. It might be noted in passing at this point that the issue of mother country-colony, or ex-colony, preferences is a highly charged one politically, a point which will be germane when the question is discussed of generalized preferences by developed to all less-developed countries, versus preferences by developed countries to selected less-developed countries. The Rome Treaty establishing the EEC almost foundered on this issue of the trade treatment to be given by the European Community as a whole to the former French colonies. In the 27th report of the Economic Committee of the League of Nations submitted in January, 1929, on the issue of most-favored-nation treatment, the following words appear: "As regards the question of preferential treatment granted to or by colonies, or to or by countries members of the same empire--a point appearing in various treaties--the Committee has refrained from investigating it in view of its political implications."

3. See, for example, Richard N. Gardner, In Pursuit of World Order (New York: Frederick A. Praeger, 1964), p. 165.

4. The United States still does grant degressive preferences, scheduled to terminate in 1974, to
the Philippines. United States preferences to Cuba
presently are dormant.

5. Numerous examples could be cited. One recent example from a highly expert source can be
found in the publication Latin American Development
and Western Hemisphere Trade, Hearings before the
Subcommittee on Inter-American Economic Relationships
of the Joint Economic Committee of the Congress of
the United States, 89th Congress, First Session, September 8-10, 1965. In the letter of August 10, 1965,
from the Inter-American Committee on the Alliance for
Progress (CIAP, from its Spanish initials) to the
Presidents of the American Republics, it is noted
that the Latin American desire for treating all developing countries alike "does not conflict with the
traditional most-favored-nation policy of the United
States." (p. 222) Walt W. Rostow, former Chairman of
the State Department's Policy Planning Council, signed
the letter as a CIAP member. The emphasis is provided.

6. Department of State message of August 18,
1923. Foreign Relations of the United States, 1923,
I, 131.

7. U.S., Statutes at Large, XLII (April,1921-
March,1923), Part 1, 944-46.

8. Memorandum of March 12, 1924, from the Economic Adviser of the Department of State to the Secretary of State. The Economic Adviser at the time
was Arthur N. Young; the memorandum was initialed by
Wallace M. McClure, a staff member.

9. An act to amend the Tariff Act of 1930,
Statutes at Large, XLVIII (March,1933-June,1934),
Part 1, 943-45. See especially Sec. 350(a).

10. There is an interesting commentary on this
in Vernon Setser, "Did Americans Originate the Conditional Most-Favored-Nation Clause?" The Journal of
Modern History, V, No. 3 (September, 1933), 319-23.
Setser concluded that "the 'conditional' principle

was formulated by French statesmen as a detail in a political plan to convince Europe and America of French unselfishness." (p. 323) Whatever the source of its invention, it was the United States for which this form became "traditional" until the 1920's.

11. The clause is Article II, Treaties, Conventions, International Acts, Protocols and Agreements between the U. S. A. and Other Powers, 1776-1909, I, 469.

12. The clause is from Article VII, Treaty Series, No. 725, p. 7.

13. The following appears in the Staff Papers presented to the Commission on Foreign Economic Policy, February, 1954, p. 256: "Thinking on this subject will be facilitated if it is understood that, on the one hand, the technical terms 'unconditional most-favored-nation treatment' and 'equality of treatment' are practically synonymous and that, on the other, the terms 'conditional most-favored-nation treatment' and 'discrimination' are close to synonymous."

14. See letter from the acting chairman of the Tariff Commission to the Secretary of State of December 14, 1922: "Our present policy is quiescent and ineffective. Advantages have come to us because it has not been carried out. To carry it out would involve us in inconsistencies, create discriminations, and result in retaliation." Foreign Relations, 1923, I, 126. The emphasis is in the original letter, but not in Foreign Relations.

15. Ibid., p. 124.

16. United States Tariff Commission, Reciprocity and Commercial Treaties (Washington: Government Printing Office, 1919), p. 10.

17. Jacob Viner, "The Most-Favored-Nation Clause in American Commercial Treaties," The Journal of Political Economy, XXXII, No. 1 (February, 1924), 111.

18. Quoted words from December 14, 1922, letter from Tariff Commission to the Secretary of State cited above, Foreign Relations, 1923, I, 122.

19. The quoted words are from the League of Nations Economic Committee, Equality of Treatment in the Present State of International Commercial Relations--The Most-Favoured-Nation Clause, Geneva, 1936, p. 8.

20. Memorandum of March 12, 1924, from the Office of the Economic Adviser to the Secretary of State, cited above.

21. U.S. Chamber of Commerce, Most-Favored-Nation Treatment and Bargaining Tariffs, Committee Report, Foreign Commerce Department, Washington, D.C., March, 1933.

22. The following are among the works which might be cited: Stanley Kuhl Hornbeck, "The Most-Favored-Nation Clause in Commercial Treaties," Bulletin of the University of Wisconsin, No. 343 (January, 1910), pp. 327-447, which is probably the most comprehensive of the studies; L. E. Visser, "La clause de la nation la plus favorisée dans les traités de commerce," Revue de Droit International, IV (1902); T. E. G. Gregory, Tariffs: A Study in Method (London: Charles Griffin & Co., Ltd., 1921); Joseph Rogers Herod, Favored Nation Treatment: An Analysis of the Most Favored Nation Clause (New York: Banks Law Publishing Co., 1901); League of Nations, Economic Committee, Equality of Treatment in the Present State of International Commercial Relations-- The Most-Favoured-Nation Clause, Geneva, 1936; Richard Riedl, Exceptions to the Most-Favoured-Nation Treatment, Report Presented to the International Chamber of Commerce (London: P. S. King & Son, Ltd., 1931). The League of Nations study cited above contains an extensive bibliography of works on the most-favored-nation policy as of 1936 (p. 26).

23. The following are some works which contain more detailed discussion of United States history with respect to tariff and most-favored-nation policy:

William Smith Culbertson, Commercial Policy in War Time and After (New York and London: D. Appleton and Co., 1924); Hugh O. Davis, America's Trade Equality Policy (Washington, D.C.: American Council on Public Affairs, 1942); Frank William Taussig, The Tariff History of the United States (8th ed.; New York: Putnam, 1931); United States Tariff Commission, Reciprocity and Commercial Treaties, op. cit., 1919; "Tariff Bargaining Under Most-Favored-Nation Treaties," letter from the Chairman of the United States Tariff Commission to the President of the Senate (Washington: Government Printing Office, 1933); Viner, op. cit.

24. GATT, BISD, 13th supplement, July, 1965, p. 100. Emphasis supplied.

25. Proceedings of the United Nations Conference on Trade and Development, Geneva, March 23-June 16, 1964. Vol. I, Final Act and Report (New York: United Nations, 1964. E/CONF.46/141, Vol. I). See especially Report of the Second Committee, pp. 143-68, particularly Paragraph 56, which refers to "most" countries favoring preferential treatment to be "extended to all developing countries uniformly." In United Nations drafting of reports of this type, the word "most" is significant. The summary records of the Second Committee also make the sentiments of most of the developing countries clear. These records are E/CONF.46/C.2.

26. UNCTAD document E/CONF.46/100, April 10, 1964.

27. Towards a New Trade Policy for Development, Report by the Secretary-General of the United Nations Conference on Trade and Development (New York: United Nations, 1964), pp. 59 ff.

28. UNCTAD document TD/B/C.2/1 and TD/B/AC.1/4 of June 4, 1965.

29. It may be useful to anticipate later discussion briefly at this point to note that while there are extremely important differences between

general and selective preferences, there also are important similarities. Even in a general preference
system, some countries are selected-out as recipients
by virtue of the arbitrary definition of what is a
less-developed country. Also, to the extent that
preferences are scaled by degree of development of
the developing countries, or by the length of time a
manufacturing establishment is in existence, this
too becomes more selective than general.

30.   James D. Richardson, A Compilation of the
Messages and Papers of the Presidents, 1789-1897
(Washington: Government Printing Office, 1896), p.
223.

31.   Speech of March 25, 1964, at Geneva. Department of State press release No. 133, March 25,
1964.

32.   "The Open System in North-South Relations,"
address of April 9, 1964, before the North Carolina
University Symposium, Chapel Hill, North Carolina.
Department of State press release No. 156, April 9,
1964. It may be worth comparing George Ball's remarks on "neo-colonialism" with a passage from Beer,
op. cit., in which Beer was describing the British
relationship with the American colonies: "The chief
positive burden which England assumed was that of imperial defence, in return for which it was considered
justifiable to restrict and mould the economic life
of the colonies." (p. 108)

33.   UNCTAD, E/CONF.46/100, April 10, 1964, p. 3.
Emphasis supplied.

34.   Towards a New Trade Policy for Development,
p. 19.

35.   Samuel Eliot Morison, The Oxford History
of the American People (New York: Oxford University
Press, 1965), p. 325.

36.   These themes are thoroughly discussed in
Taussig, op. cit.

37.   Hornbeck, op. cit., p. 348.

38.   There also is a feeling among many American businessmen that it is not businessmen in less-developed countries who are seeking trade preferences, but rather the government officials of these countries.   American businessmen frequently also discount much of the noise and clamor accompanying the request for preferences.   One joke heard at a meeting illustrative of this concerned an advertisement seen by an importer of leather offering frog skins in lots of 1,000 at a phenomenally low price.   After making the order, the importer received a small envelope containing only three skins and a brief note stating: "From the noise, it sounded as though there were a lot more."

39.   U.S. Department of State, "American Commercial Policy, with Particular Reference to the Most-Favored-Nation Clause (1620-1923)," Research Project No. 725, August 1965, Historical Studies Division, Historical Office, Bureau of Public Affairs, p. 7. (Unpublished.)

40.   Memorandum of March 12, 1924, from the Office of the Economic Adviser to the Secretary of State, op. cit.

41.   Foreign Relations, 1923, I, 131.

42.   Reciprocity and Commercial Treaties, op. cit.

43.   Address of the President of the United States delivered at a Joint Session of the Two Houses of Congress, January 8, 1918, Foreign Relations of the United States, 1918; Supplement 1:   The World War, I, 15.   Gottfried Haberler, in his The Theory of International Trade (New York: Macmillan, 1936), has noted that this is an unconditional form of the most-favored-nation clause advocated before the actual U.S. policy shift in 1923 (p. 363).

44.   Jacob Viner, The Customs Union Issue (New York: Carnegie Endowment for International Peace, 1950), p. 18.

45. Benjamin H. Williams, Economic Foreign Policy of the United States (New York: McGraw-Hill, 1929), pp. 307 ff.

46. Ibid., p. 321.

47. Thomas A. Bailey, A Diplomatic History of the American People (6th ed.; New York: Appleton, 1958), p. 2.

48. Foreign Relations, 1899, pp. 128-42.

49. R. W. Green, "Commonwealth Preference: Tariff Duties and Preferences on United Kingdom Exports to the Preference Area," Board of Trade Journal, CLXXXVIII, No. 3560 (June 11, 1965).

50. BISD, Sixth Supplement, March, 1958, p. 96.

51. It has become an accepted cliché among those following these matters that the Commonwealth preference system is fading away over time. This may be less than accurate, as can be seen from the Board of Trade study of U.K. exports cited above: "Comparisons with an earlier study suggest that though there has been some erosion of margins since 1948 in many markets, the decline in the value of preference on our exports to the Area as a whole which occurred between 1937 and 1948 has not continued at the same pace in the following decade." Green, op. cit., p. iv.

52. The New York Times, November 27, 1965, reported that the focus of the OECD meeting on trade with underdeveloped countries "was on the urging of the United States." The Journal of Commerce, in an article on December 2, 1965, by Richard Lawrence of its Washington bureau, referred to the "spheres of influence factor" as being one of the motivations of the United States in requesting the study, although he did not argue that this was its main purpose.

53. Latin American Development and Western Hemisphere Trade, op. cit., pp. 158-59.

54. That this assistance program in Africa is not necessarily popular in France is discussed in an article by Philippe Decraene, "France's Changing Policy in Africa," The Reporter, XXXIV, No. 1 (January 13, 1966), 37-39.

55. John Pincus, Economic Aid and International Cost Sharing (Santa Monica, California: The RAND Corporation, 1965), p. 143. This book also has been published by The Johns Hopkins Press, Baltimore, Maryland, 1965.

56. Washington Post, December 14, 1965. Lippmann is over-simplifying terribly, since France obviously feels a kinship with Africa and England with Commonwealth countries which are not "Western." But even with this oversimplification, Lippmann is discussing a real phenomenon in United States-Latin American relations.

57. Samuel Flagg Bemis, A Diplomatic History of the United States (4th ed.; New York: Holt, Rinehart and Winston, 1955), p. 732.

58. Blaine's role is discussed briefly in Willis Fletcher Johnson, An American Statesman: The Works and Words of James G. Blaine (Augusta Publishing Co., 1892), pp. 521-25. United States-Latin American preferences also are discussed in Taussig, op. cit.

59. This and subsequent references to decisions of the Conference come from the Minutes of the International American Conference, Washington, D.C., October 2, 1889-April 19, 1890.

60. From a speech before the American Chamber of Commerce of Mexico, Mexico City, April 5, 1965, cited in Latin American Development and Western Hemisphere Trade, op. cit., p. 216.

61. Samuel Flagg Bemis, The Latin American Policy of the United States (New York: Harcourt, Brace and Co., 1943).

62. Committee for Economic Development, _Trade Negotiations for a Better Free World Economy_, May, 1964, p. 41.

63. Henry S. Reuss, _The Critical Decade_ (New York: McGraw-Hill Book Co., 1964), Chap. 2.

64. Randall Hinshaw, _The European Community and American Trade_, published for the Council on Foreign Relations (paperback; New York: Frederick A. Praeger, 1964), final chapter.

65. The proposal is reproduced in _Latin American Development and Western Hemisphere Trade_, _op. cit._, p. 170.

CHAPTER **3** SOME CONCEPTS
UNDERLYING THE
PREFERENCE IDEAS

Various philosophical, theoretical, as well as
practical, considerations often are cited by proponents of trade preferences for manufactured goods by
developed to less-developed countries. The purpose
of this chapter is to examine some of these.

THE MEANING OF EQUALITY

Preference ideas are not unique to the trade
field. And what is "equal" and what is "preferential" treatment often depends on the vision of the
beholder. The abstraction "equality" takes on operational meaning only when a particular form of it is
applied in practice. Farmers consider that agricultural price supports give them equality with other
sectors of the population; oil companies argue that
depletion allowances provide equality by compensat-
ing for risk. In a sense, equality refers to the
perquisites one receives; privilege is what others
receive.

The purpose of this philosophic digression is
merely to indicate why the poorest nations, those
generally doing least well in international trade,
wish to change the prevailing notion about trade
"equality." Equality, they argue, will come only
when the poorest are given preferred treatment.

The most-favored-nation clause has its social
and political and even juridical counterparts. With
respect to the Negro rights problem in the United
States, President Johnson has said:

> You do not take a person who, for
> years, has been hobbled by chains and
> liberate him, bring him up to the
> starting line of a race and then say,
> "you are free to compete with all the
> others," and still justly believe that
> you have been completely fair.
>
> Thus it is not enough just to open
> the gates of opportunity. All our cit-
> izens must have the ability to walk
> through those gates.
>
> This is the next and the more pro-
> found stage of the battle for civil
> rights. We seek not just freedom but
> opportunity. We seek not just legal
> equity but human ability--not just
> equality as a right and a theory, but
> equality as a fact and equality as a
> result.[1]

Anatole France has expressed the issue well:
"The law, in its majestic equality, forbids the rich
as well as the poor to sleep under bridges, to beg
in the streets, and to steal bread."[2]

The same issue arose in recent correspondence
between Attorney General Nicholas Katzenbach and
United States Appeals Court Chief Judge in the Dis-
trict of Columbia, David Bazelon, regarding criminal
procedures suggested by the American Law Institute
for the questioning of suspects. Judge Bazelon argued that the proposed procedures discriminated un-
fairly against the poor and the Negroes. The Attorney General replied that the purpose of criminal investigation is not to insure equal treatment but to
discover those guilty of crime.[3]

These are the same family of issues raised by
trade preference ideas. Myrdal makes the point that
the most-favored-nation principle of the GATT is an
equitable one: "It is an ideal that they [all na-
tions] should be equal but if, in fact, they are
not, equal treatment becomes inequality." He cites
Sir N. Raghavan Pillai, Indian Under Secretary of

Foreign Affairs: "Equality of treatment is equitable
only among equals."[4]

The unconditional most-favored-nation principle
has at least two tremendous advantages as being the
most equitable way of treating all nations in international trade: It is the current doctrine; and it
is simple.   Once one departs from this simplicity,
inequality has to be defined on arbitrary grounds
and then arbitrarily compensated for.   Are only the
rich to be forbidden to sleep under bridges?   How
many gradations of "poor" nations are there, or is
inequality only a matter of two classes, the rich
and the poor?

But the major point is that the definition of
equality is challenged because all is not well.
Freeing Negro slaves did not give them equal opportunity; identical right to counsel and arraignment
procedures does not result in equal treatment for
rich and poor.   The poor nations are not doing as
well in international trade as the richer ones, and
they wish to do better.   They therefore wish to re-
define equality.

INDUSTRIALIZATION AND DEVELOPMENT

It has become commonplace in recent economic
literature to accept as given the fact that poor
countries want to industrialize.   The acceptance at
times seems grudging.   Harry Johnson has presented a
theory of commercial policy which assumes a "preference for industrial production"; he then states that
this preference comprises "the effects of electoral
ignorance and the influence of power groups on government policy."[5]   Cooper and Massell accept industrialization as a legitimate policy goal, and then
proceed in their analysis from the assumption that
the formation of what they call "industry" is preferred even at a greater cost than nonindustrial
production.[6]

There is no reason to quarrel with either of

the two analyses cited except as illustrations of a
bias which tends to creep into their assumptions,
namely, that policy-makers want industrialization,
regardless of whether industrialization is "rational"
or "irrational." The Cooper-Massell analysis pro-
claims itself as static, and therefore makes no
claims about the goodness or badness of industrialization as a dynamic proposition. But it is precisely this dynamic aspect that motivates economists
from less-developed countries. They want industrialization not because they "prefer" it in some abstract
sense, but because they see little hope for development (a dynamic process) in its absence. This is
not to say that agriculture need be neglected in
order to industrialize; but rather that in most tropical countries, there is a limit to the growth of
export proceeds from tropical agricultural products
and a limit to their earning capacity in foreign
markets for temperate-zone agricultural products.
The low price and income elasticities of demand for
such key tropical agricultural products as coffee
and cocoa, which is the argument used by many economists from less-developed countries to justify the
need for industrialization, is well known and need
not be repeated.

The Economic Commission for Latin America, when
it was under the direction of Raúl Prebisch, was an
important stimulator of industrialization, using the
import-substitution route, in Latin America.[7] However, ECLA should not be given all the credit (or
blame, depending on one's viewpoint) for this industrialization, since ECLA largely advocated, and provided the theoretical underpinning for, what the
political leaders of the Latin American countries
wanted to do anyhow. The industrialization of the
United States, itself an agricultural country par
excellence, is illustrative of the same drive for
industry; and, the United States case is an example
that industrialization need not be at the cost of
sacrificing agriculture. Agriculture did suffer in
the Latin American case in the sense of inadequate
growth, in part due to the belief that industry was
good, and that agriculture therefore was bad.

Hopefully, this sort of adversary relationship between industry and agriculture is now less prevalent; the more logical argument would seem to be that increased agricultural productivity may be a necessary path to industrialization.

The relevant point for a discussion of preferences for manufactured goods is that the less-developed countries are convinced that some industrialization is necessary for adequate economic growth for most of them. Maizels has made this point in his massive study on world trade in manufactures: "Though industrialization may not be the appropriate policy for economic growth in every country, it seems that in many--probably the majority--of the less-developed countries, industrialization is the key to economic progress."[8] The United States has committed itself to help in the industrialization of Latin American countries in the charter of Punta del Este. Prebisch, in his new capacity as Secretary-General of UNCTAD, still believes in "the absolute necessity of building up trade in industrial exports" if the developing countries are to close what he calls their "trade gap."[9] Prebisch's basis for this "absolute necessity" is his analysis of the deterioration of the terms of trade of primary commodity exporters.

The preamble to the Final Act of UNCTAD contains the following paragraph:

> The developing countries should not
> rely merely on the expansion of tradi-
> tional exports of primary products and
> raw materials. Promotion of industries
> with an export potential in developing
> countries is essential. Diversifica-
> tion and expansion of exports of manu-
> factured and semi-manufactured goods
> are among the important means to as-
> sist the developing countries to achieve
> in time a balance in their external
> accounts.[10]

Finally, it might be noted that the United Nations General Assembly in December, 1965, approved a resolution establishing "an autonomous organization for the promotion of industrial development to be known as the United Nations Organization for Industrial Development," culminating an institutional effort of the developing countries that had been in progress for many years.[11]

The economic analysis of whether some degree of industrialization, or at least some degree of processing of raw materials and thereby adding value domestically, is essential for rapid economic growth, presumably depends on the natural endowments of a country, the price and particularly income elasticities of demand for its raw materials, the diversity of its raw materials, its own supply elasticities, and the like. The belief of this writer is that for practically all countries, a stage will be reached in their development when a degree of industrialization, broadly defined to include domestic processing of primary products, will be necessary for sustained growth. All less-developed countries have not reached that stage; some have.

And, in this last fact, lies an important point of the pressure for trade preferences for manufactures and semimanufactures. It comes from those underdeveloped countries which, for better or worse, have some industrial establishment in being, and which are committed to further industrialization. Some of them have neglected their agriculture-- shamefully, in the opinion of the writer--in the process of industrialization, but this point is not really relevant to the discussion of preferences for manufactured goods. Thus India, Brazil, Argentina, Yugoslavia, the United Arab Republic, Pakistan, have been in the forefront of the drive for preferences. Most of the countries in Africa, which have not yet reached the stage of very much industrialization, seem to be less immediately excited about this issue.

The point is an important one for a policy-maker; when it is alleged that the underdeveloped

countries are aligned solidly to convince the United
States to give preferences, this really means that
some underdeveloped countries, those listed above
and a few others, want preferences. Other underdeveloped countries are presently indifferent, since
they have nothing to lose and may perhaps gain some
day. And still others, those which now have preferences on a selective basis and which would have to
share these if they were generalized to all countries defined as underdeveloped, tend to favor only
those preference systems which have gradations by
level of development.

If one accepts the desirability of some industrialization in countries such as Brazil and Argentina, to name only two, the issue is not really
whether preferences would or would not help, say,
Upper Volta as well--but whether preferences would
help Brazil's and Argentina's industrialization; and
at what cost, if any, to Upper Volta, to others, and
to Brazil and Argentina. To be of great value, any
discussion must be on essentially dynamic terms--
what new industries might be formed, what existing
industries might be encouraged to expand, what foreign private capital flows to less-developed countries would be fostered, if there were preferences?
Are there alternatives to preferences? Since countries rarely give something for nothing, what would
be the price of preferences?

The foregoing role of preferences as an aid to
industrialization treats of the dynamics of the issue. It was this dynamic aspect that Prebisch prop-
erly stressed in his <u>Towards a New Trade Policy for
Development</u> as being the crucial aspect.

> The case for preferential treatment for
> exports of developing countries is that
> it would help the industries of devel-
> oping countries to overcome the diffi-
> culties that they encounter in export
> markets because of their high initial
> costs. . . . The case is thus a logi-
> cal extension of the infant industry
> argument.[12]

Writers also have focused on the resource transfer, or aid, component of preferences.[13] If one
makes a series of assumptions, this aspect at least
permits a stab at quantification. These quantifica-
tions of resource transfers are essentially static
approaches. They provide a different technique for
giving foreign aid and, in this sense, really do not
appear to be very exciting for the less-developed
countries, particularly if this form of aid were to
replace other forms.

These issues will be discussed in greater detail at the appropriate points. What should be kept
in mind is that the interesting issue is that of
preferences as a spur to industrialization, which is
dynamic and not easily quantifiable. And the less
interesting issue is the static one, where efforts
at quantification, which do not appear to be of terribly great importance, have been made.

THE QUESTION OF SCALE

In addition to the need for industrialization
by many developing countries, "come what may,"[14]
there also seems to be a strong belief among their
leaders that effective industrialization requires
principally large-scale industries. That economies
of scale work almost across-the-board, and in almost all industries, seems to be built into their
thinking. From time to time, the Europeans reach
the same conclusions regarding their competition
with the United States; that is, since American companies tend to be bigger than European, competition
between the two may not be fair. The poor countries
almost uniformly believe the same thing--that their
industries must be bigger if they are to be competitive.

There are unlimited examples which may be cited
to support the contention that developing countries
are deeply preoccupied with the question of scale.
Unfortunately, the preoccupation normally is highly
imprecise.

In dealing with dynamic comparative cost advantages, UNCTAD made a special point of stressing the size of the domestic markets of developing countries since this, it was felt, "may be helpful in realizing the full benefits of economies of scale in the shortest possible period."[15] In dealing with the promotion of trade in manufactures among developing countries, one of the very first points cited in the relevant UNCTAD recommendation was to note "the great advantages of economies of scale and specialization offered by modern technology."[16]

There are at least three different levels on which one might think about economies of scale: the plant level; the level of the company; the level of the country. The conclusions might be different depending on the level one has in mind. Thus, if one were to argue that underdeveloped countries are unable to compete in world bicycle or world toy trade, to pick only two industries which already exist in many of these countries, this does not seem to be a matter of plant size, or even of company size. It may be a bit more relevant to the size of the country doing the exporting, since scale questions, as will be noted, involve more than lumpy investment in fixed capital. In the automobile industry in Latin America, for example, it would be inaccurate to say that the total market of the Latin American Free-Trade Association is too small to support an automobile industry; it probably is true that the LAFTA market is too small to support as many small plants as there now are. In this case, the economies of scale may well relate to the minimum investment needed at the plant level for a given efficient output of automobiles.[17]

In a recent discussion in The Economist (London), the issues of trade preferences and economies of scale were thoroughly mixed together because of a failure to differentiate between heavy and light industries and between plant and country levels when dealing with the scale question. The article discussed the Latin American industrialization process as starting in the heavy industry field; it discussed

the Latin American automobile industry at some
length as a case where there are too many small
plants, each making too small assembly runs, for
the industry to be competitive in world markets.
And then, almost without transition, the article
recommended "a system of export favours or permitted export subsidies for the infant industries of
developing countries" in order that "infant firms in
developing countries are encouraged to grow to their
proper economic size."18

Despite the fact that some token exports might
earn some foreign exchange, it certainly would not
seem to be in the automobile industry that the
world's poor countries should be encouraged to compete at this stage of their development in the markets of the developed countries. Yet this seems to
be precisely what The Economist is recommending.
The issue of plant scale is relevant to the Latin
American automobile industry; it is relevant to
Latin American economic integration. But the Latin
American automobile industry is not relevant to a
discussion of tariff preferences by rich to poor
countries at this stage of world history.

This last point is of some interest in seeking
to understand precisely what it is that the poor
countries want from their preference proposals. The
poor countries are seeking some present trading advantages in order to develop industries which they
hope will have some long-term comparative advantage,
and for which a certain amount of time will be needed
for the industries to develop sufficient efficiency
to compete without the preferences. This may be an
issue of scale; but it is just as likely not to be.
It is more likely to be an issue of other forms of
economies.

The industries in which developing countries
may be able to compete under a system of tariff preferences are not now likely to be those in which the
richer countries are most efficient. The export industries likely to be more promising for the less-
developed countries are those which, possibly in

combination with advanced technology, exploit the one factor--labor--in which poor countries are likely to have a present advantage; and these may not be industries where scale is a crucial factor.

It is easy to find conflicting views among economists on the issue of scale. Viner, in dealing with the subject from the plant-level viewpoint, argued that there probably are manufacturing industries where scale is vital, but probably only few. "There are few industries, even in countries where large-scale production is common, in which there are not plants of moderate size which are as efficient, or nearly as efficient, measured in unit-costs, as the giant plants."[19] Viner also argued that "it does not seem probable that the prospects of reduction in unit-costs of production as the result of enlargement of the tariff area are ordinarily substantial, even when the individual member countries are quite small in economic size."[20] This last quotation melds the plant- and country-size aspects of scale.

Gardner Patterson has noted, regarding economies of scale, that "it has become a virtual article of faith among many of those responsible for determining policy [of developing countries] that such phenomena are widespread."[21] Patterson states that there probably are instances in less-developed countries where important economies of scale are possible, but he seems to stress more the related issue of external economies, which may be absent at an early stage of development and then become more available as development proceeds, as more crucial to promoting less-developed country exports than scale per se.

Prebisch, in his Towards a New Trade Policy for Development, has focused much on the small size of countries and their low per capita incomes.[22] He has argued that these facts, plus the need for industrialization "come what may" in many of these countries, has led to sheltered, small-scale domestic industries, unable to compete in world markets, and that

preferential export trade is one avenue of escape
from this. What Prebisch seems to be saying is that
preferences will provide a form of incentive and
competition, by forcing companies to seek sales in
developed countries, that will permit industries of
sufficient scale to develop in the poor countries.

A point of some interest overlooked in the
Prebisch analysis is that the main advocates of
preferences are not the small countries of the type
cited, but the large countries such as India, which,
inter alia, are seeking techniques to earn sufficient foreign exchange to optimize the import component of production and to optimally utilize industrial capacity.

The purpose of this present discussion is not
necessarily to reach conclusions, but hopefully to
clarify issues. The following are among the points
which seem worth keeping in mind.

There undoubtedly are industries in which economies of scale exist and in which less-developed
countries are unable to produce cheaply because of
the insufficient scale of their industries. The
automobile industry, chemical fertilizers, paper and
pulp, steel, and other similar industries come to
mind as probably being of this type. The economies
of scale relate in part to optimum plant size for
production, and in part to company size for services
related to production, such as purchase of goods and
services as inputs, sales force, publicity, economy
of over-all management, and the like. However,
these are unlikely to be the industries in which the
less-developed countries could benefit at present
from trade preferences from the industrialized countries in order to expand to the required scale.
These are precisely the industries in which the richer countries are efficient. Since preferences will
give the poor-country producer no advantage over
domestic producers in rich countries, these are
therefore the industries in which the poor countries
for the most part will have to compete on equal
terms in the world's major markets, such as the
United States, the EEC, EFTA, and Japan. And such
successful competition really is not in the cards.

However, these are the industries in which economic integration among less-developed countries could give large payoffs. It is in these industries that LAFTA is having great difficulty, and where the promise is immense.

The kinds of industries in which preferences in the developed-country markets would seem to be most promising for the less-developed countries are those where scale may count up to a point, but where scale is unlikely to be crucial in and of itself. The toy industry, bicycles, small motors, sewing machines, processing of domestic agricultural products such as oilseeds, may be examples of such industries. These industries may require a reasonable size to be both competitive and profitable, but this is not the size that less-developed countries have in mind when referring to economies of large-scale production.

The issue of external economies, the need to develop infrastructure, domestic technical skills, and the like, is related to scale, but is more a function of degree of development of a country. This, as Patterson seems to argue, would appear to be a more important aspect of the preference issue than is scale.

The question of size of country and the need for exports--the issue raised by Prebisch--undoubtedly is germane to the preference issue. Many writers have noted the correlation between population and exports, namely, that the foreign trade/ national income ratio tends to be lower the greater the population; and they have noted the greater importance of foreign trade to small than to large countries.[23] This is a form of scale issue, but of scale related to a country and its income rather than of scale related to plant or company size. This, of course, is not an argument that large countries, particularly poor large countries with a paucity of foreign exchange, do not also have to rely heavily on trade in the development process.

What the evidence does seem to indicate is that countries with smaller populations need to trade more, relatively in terms of per capita incomes, than big ones. And since the great bulk of the less-developed countries are small, there is some support for the contention that they should be helped in some way to expand their trade. But quite clearly, at this point of history, the potential beneficiaries of preferences would not be the very small countries but rather those with larger populations, viz., India, Pakistan, Mexico, etc.

This is not necessarily an argument in favor of preferences in developed country markets, since there may be other techniques (some of which will be discussed in this study) to expand the trade of poor countries. But this issue certainly is relevant to the preference discussion--just as automobile preferences are not really relevant. Also, this is not the simple argument that trade and development are themselves correlated, without regard to the size and gross national product of a nation. As will be seen, the simple argument that the greater a country's exports, the greater its development will be-- which spokesmen from less-developed countries sometimes make--is not supported by the facts.

EXPORT MARKETS AND NATIONAL MARKETS

Economists are not in agreement whether the major engine of growth for countries is, or is likely to be in the future, the development of national or of export markets. Nor are they in agreement about which should come first--the development of the national market, leading from there into the export field, or the development of both markets simultaneously in order to take advantage of economies of scale. If one talks of manufacturing automobiles in, say, Paraguay, obviously the domestic market alone would be inadequate. But if one talks of the more realistic world of producing consumer and light producer goods in, say, Mexico, then it may be that the national market should come first and the export market flow out of this.

The issue is not a simple one, and there obviously are variations industry by industry and country by country, but the central issue is one of some interest to the preference discussion. A central theme of Prebisch's paper, Towards a New Trade Policy for Development, is that national markets cannot be exploited in many less-developed countries in the absence of expanded exports.[24] His case rests on limited domestic markets and the need for economies of scale.

Rostow has taken a different viewpoint. In a series of speeches in recent years, he has discussed what he calls the concept of the "national market." What this involves is the modernization of agriculture, better domestic marketing techniques, and most important, the rectification in favor of the rural sector of the domestic terms of trade so that the farmer can become a customer of the city manufacturer, and the city dweller a good customer of the farmer. As this process develops, he argues that exports follow: "Historically the export of manufactured goods has usually followed or paralleled the development of a national market."[25]

In dealing with United States growth in the period 1790-1860, North has argued that the export sector was the major stimulus for growth.[26] North focused not only on exports, but more importantly, on their character, and their forward and backward linkage effects. Thus, the nature of the exports from the South (tobacco and later cotton) and the lack of stress on education under the plantation system of the region, did not encourage growth. The nature of Northern and Western exports, on the other hand, did promote growth. North draws heavily in his analysis on the backward and forward linkage ideas of Hirschman.[27] These references to North and Hirschman are made largely to indicate that their focus is more on the nature of a country's industry and other endowments, and the effects of their exploitation, rather than on the export versus the national market question. This is true despite the central theme of North on exports as an engine of development in the American case.

Nurkse has argued that export-led growth seems
to be a thing of the past.[28]

ECLA, presumably reflecting in part the attitude of Prebisch, has articulated the idea that
growth depends on imports, imports depend on exports, and hence that growth depends on exports.
Prebisch makes this multiple causation quite explicit in Towards a New Trade Policy for Development:

> First and foremost, it should not be
> expected that, if the income of all de-
> veloping countries is to rise at the
> minimum by 5 per cent every year, their
> imports can increase at a rate much
> less than 6 per cent. . . . The second
> implication of the 5 per cent growth
> target is that exports of the develop-
> ing countries would also have to rise
> at the rate of 6 per cent per annum,
> in order to maintain balance-of-payments
> equilibrium. More precisely, a volume
> of exports should rise at a rate which,
> after allowing for changes in the terms
> of trade, would pay for a volume of im-
> ports increasing each year at a rate of
> 6 per cent.[29]

Using ECLA data, the average annual rates of
growth in gross domestic product of selected Latin
American countries from 1952 to 1964 were 1.6 per
cent for Argentina, 5.4 per cent for Brazil, 4.1 per
cent for Chile, 4.7 per cent for Colombia, 5.3 per
cent for Mexico, and 6.6 per cent for Venezuela.
These growth rates seem to bear no correlation with
export growth. Indeed, Brazil, whose growth rate
was high, actually had a decline in exports since
the early 1950's; Argentina and Chile have had the
highest per capita exports, and Mexico and Brazil
the lowest. Venezuela, which had an extremely high
level of exports, clearly is a special case.

The conclusions which seem to emerge are that
while the ratio of exports to national income seems

to be negatively correlated with the population of a
country, there is no simple correlation (at least
over a ten-year span in Latin America) between exports and domestic growth rates. (It may of course
be argued that domestic growth unaccompanied by increased exports is unsustainable for most countries
and that in this sense export expansion is necessary
for growth.) While one can work out a global comparison between total product growth rates and the
rates of growth both of exports and imports--which is
what Prebisch presumably has done--this has little
meaning for specific countries and becomes no more
than a statistical exercise for them.

If exports are not necessarily or always the
main engine of growth, is industry such an engine?
Again, it would seem to depend on the industries and
the countries. In the case of Venezuela, a primary
product, petroleum, has been that engine. In the
case of the Midwest at an earlier stage of American
history, it was, _inter alia_, an agricultural product,
grain. In the more recent cases of Australia and
New Zealand, it was agriculture. In the case of
Mexico, as Rostow has argued, it was the development
of the national market.

The purpose of this discussion is to reflect
skepticism of the easy assumption that as exports
rise, self-sustaining economic growth must necessarily follow. It all depends. The intent of the discussion also is to cast doubt on the use of global
figures showing the behavior of imports, exports,
and growth, since these may or may not mean anything
in specific cases. It is not the purpose of this
discussion to argue that exports don't count; they
obviously do and they obviously are the main source
for foreign exchange for capital and raw material
imports if industrialization is to take place. But
exports are not necessarily the only source of foreign exchange. Some figures on this point will be
given subsequently.

It is not the purpose of this study to analyze
foreign aid, or to compare aid in all its ramifications with trade in all its ramifications, or to

suggest reversion to an earlier slogan in United States foreign economic policy of "trade not aid." However, it may be useful to touch on the issue of the relative efficacies of industrial exports versus foreign aid in just one respect. In a one-for-one comparison, aid obviously is superior to exports from a resource viewpoint, since $1 of grant aid costs the recipient nothing, whereas $1 of exports requires the sacrifice of some resource. But in another qualitative sense, the export is superior since a competitive industry may have been necessary to effect this. ("May have been" since subsidies or similar devices may have facilitated the export.) It has been argued that the preference technique, working through exports, is self-policing in that the country succeeds in getting foreign exchange through a system of preferences only if it exports; it may be able to get the foreign exchange without the self-policing measures through aid.[30]

This may be one of the stronger arguments in favor of trade preferences, namely, since they are self-policing and will work for any particular less-developed country only if it out-competes other countries (some enjoying preferences, some not) in export markets, preferences would tend to encourage efficient allocation of resources. On the other hand, import substitution and high tariffs to protect infant domestic industries need not encourage efficient resource allocation since such industries need never compete to stay alive. Neither argument-- that infant-industry import protection may promote inefficient resource allocation while export preferences are more likely to result in efficient allocation--should be pushed too far since enough exceptions can be found to both generalizations. But, on a priori reasoning, there is no reason to believe that preferences will foster inefficient allocation of resources.

THE TRADE GAP

UNCTAD has popularized the gap way of looking at the trade needs of the developing countries. The

gap can be approached in various ways. The way used
by the United Nations, and cited by Prebisch in Towards a New Policy for Development, was to start out
with the 5 per cent per annum growth target of the
Development Decade; then to make some assumptions
about the growth in imports, particularly of investment goods which cannot be produced domestically in
less-developed countries, required to achieve this
rate (the assumption was 6 per cent a year); then
make some further assumptions about the future trend
of exports by less-developed countries; and from
this come out with a total gap.[31]

The gap figure on current account estimated by
the United Nations was $20 billion a year by 1970.
The United Nations' estimate further assumed that by
1970 the net inflow to the developing countries of
long-term capital and official donations would be $9
billion a year, leaving a remaining gap on both current and capital account of $11 billion a year.

In order to understand what much of the discussion at UNCTAD was all about, it is important to know
the use to which this $20-billion-a-year trade gap
was put; and also to know some of the limiting assumptions behind it.

Prebisch made the trade gap the theme of UNCTAD.
"This, then, has to be the starting-point of the
Conference. One cannot posit a 5 per cent rate of
development without accepting also all the consequences that this implies for the rates of growth of
imports and exports."[32] The $20 billion trade-gap
figure figures prominently in the Preamble to the
Final Act of UNCTAD.[33] The gap idea tends to be repeated almost parrot-like by spokesmen from developing countries. And the figure $20 billion a year
similarly has become something of an accepted fact
by them.

The gap, as used at UNCTAD, has its limitations.
It deals only with current account (and was called a
trade gap). Thus, if past trends of long-term capital movement continue, even the United Nations

estimate of the residual gap in 1970 is reduced to
$11 billion.

Much more importantly, the gap figure assumes
that the future will be a replica of the past. If
this is inaccurate--if imports, exports, services,
or all these, change--the figure loses meaning. If
total long-term capital movements alter, the current
and capital account gap will alter.

If (a) all the assumptions turn out to be accurate, and (b) the future is a replica of the past,
and (c) the gap is not filled--then the result must
be not a gap, since this is an abstract concept, but
growth of less than 5 per cent a year on the average
until 1970. If the 5 per cent a year growth target
is met, by definition there can be no gap. In a
sense, the reasoning thus becomes self-defeating.
The premise, an average growth rate of 5 per cent a
year, if achieved, would result in no gap; the gap
will result only if the premise is invalid. Prebisch
may be cited on this point:

> This gap is potential and not real: if
> the means of bridging the gap are not
> found, the developing countries will be
> forced to reduce their rates of growth
> unless they are prepared to achieve
> higher rates at an excessive economic
> and social cost involving serious po-
> litical consequences.[34]

The gap has another major defect; it is a global figure for all countries taken together. And a
global gap, even if the figure were precisely accurate as a projection, has no meaning in a practical
sense for a given country. The gap concept has been
used frequently in the past, e.g., in projecting
country balance-of-payments deficits in the Marshall
Plan, and since, but it achieves some operational
significance only when applied to a specific program
of a specific country. In other words, the gap is
useful as a planning device--or as a propaganda device for a world development conference--but not as
a precise reality.

The global gap also omits the point made earlier, namely, that the correlation between growth in
domestic product and imports and exports may have
some statistical validity for the world or given
regions of the world taken as a whole, but has no
real meaning over any reasonable time span for individual countries.

It is not worth belaboring the gap, except to
keep it in perspective. Estimators (gapoligists)
other than the United Nations have had their try at
gap figures. Balassa estimated a current account
gap of around $12 billion for 1970.[35] There are
several other estimates as well.[36]

While any figures of global trade gaps have
only limited practical usefulness, what lies behind
these predictive efforts to forecast the value of
imports not covered by exports is of considerable
importance in seeking to understand the trade problems faced by the less-developed countries.[37]

The relatively poorer performance in the last
ten to fifteen years of the developing countries,
compared either with the so-called developed-market
economies (North America, Western Europe, Australia,
New Zealand, Japan, South Africa) or the centrally
planned countries (the United Nations' euphemism for
the Communist countries) is well known, but might
nevertheless bear some summarization.[38]

The average annual growth in exports from
1950-62 was 8.0 per cent for the developed-market
economies, 11.1 per cent for the centrally planned
economies, and only 3.4 per cent for the developing-
market economies. That is, the poorest countries
had by far the lowest growth rates. The situation
did improve somewhat in 1963 and 1964, as can be
seen from Table 2.

In 1950, the developing countries exported 32
per cent of the value of world exports; by 1962,
this figure was down to 21 per cent. Indeed, in
each and every year but one between 1953 and 1963,

the share of total world trade of what the GATT calls
the nonindustrial countries was less than the year
before.[39] The one exception was that in both 1962
and 1963, the shares were 24 per cent. From the
viewpoint of the poor countries, there clearly is
something amiss with the pattern of world trade when
they fare worse than any other group in both absolute and percentage growth of exports, particularly
at a time when they feel the reverse should be the
case.

TABLE 2

Year-to-Year Rates of Growth of Exports,
Per Cent Increase over Previous Year

	Developed Market Economies	Centrally Planned Economies	Developing Market Economies
1961	6	4	1
1962	5	11	5
1963	9	7	9
1964	13	7	8

Source: United Nations,Economic and Social Council,
         World Economic Survey, 1964: Part II,
         Chapter 1, Table 1-5.

A few other figures might be cited to understand
the motivation of the developing countries in empha-
sizing trade at this point in history, and in focusing on preferences for manufactured goods.

Using United Nations' figures, export earnings
of the developing countries in 1964 were $34 billion.

The export-earning figure in 1963 had been slightly
more than $31 billion. As noted earlier, the rate
of increase in export earnings of these countries
has been higher in recent years than in the late
1950's, about 5.6 per cent a year between 1960 and
1964 as compared with half that rate earlier.

By contrast with these trade earnings, again
using United Nations' figures, the net flow of long-
term capital and official donations from developed
countries and multilateral agencies to the developing countries was about $7.5 billion in 1963. The
annual average for the years 1960-63 was about $6.8
billion. These figures include private as well as
official capital movements.

The foregoing data on long-term capital flows
are necessarily imprecise since capital flight from
developing to developed countries is not taken into
account in the foregoing "net" concept; in addition,
other flows from centrally planned economies are not
included. Nevertheless, the magnitude involved is
the significant figure.

The comparison, therefore, of foreign-exchange
availabilities of the developing countries in 1963
was roughly $31 to $32 billion from trade and about
$7.5 billion from long-term capital movements, both
aid and private investment. Even this $7.5 billion
figure is overstated, since as Pincus points out,
it gives equal weight to grants, loans of all terms
and conditions, contributions in kind, etc.[40] Trade
clearly is more important than aid as a generator of
foreign exchange for developing countries.

Furthermore, the rate of increase in the net
flow of capital resources to the developing countries
slowed down from the late 1950's to the early 1960's
from the rate during the period of the first to the
second half of the 1950's. Of the total flow, it is
also significant that private capital seems to have
played a smaller role in the 1960's than in the second half of the 1950's. Taking these two facts in
conjunction--the slowing down of the rate of growth

of the total flow of resources, and the slowing down even more of private capital flows--and combining them with what developing countries interpret as the mood of the parliaments of the rich countries to cut aid budgets even in absolute terms--one can easily see the basis for the greater interest of the developing countries in trade than aid. The trade paydirt seems bigger and more promising. This is in addition to the fact that earning one's way by trade may be less demeaning psychologically than receiving aid.

The preference issue relates to manufactured and processed goods; except for those countries which now enjoy preferred markets for primary products, the goal for trade in this field is to eliminate tariffs and thus eliminate all preferences. There is obviously a differential interest among less-developed countries on this focus on manufactured goods. Those less-developed countries that have manufacturing industries in being are in the forefront of the drive for preferences; those that have no manufacturing industries are indifferent and devote their attention more to primary commodity trade.

This is not the place to review the familiar arguments of why export growth has been and is likely to continue to be slow for certain key primary-product exports such as coffee and cocoa; or why the export of minerals, without some industrialization that goes beyond mere exploitation, minimizes the forward and backward linkage effects conducive to growth. It need merely be noted that developing countries are deeply aware of the problems of primary-commodity trade; are deeply concerned about their present excessive export dependence on a narrow range of primary commodities; and are pressing in various ways and in many forums for some amelioration of the problems associated with primary-commodity trade. UNCTAD set up a committee on commodities of the Trade and Development Board to deal with this range of issues; the International Bank for Reconstruction and Development recently issued

a report on supplemental financial measures to deal
with problems arising from unexpected adverse movements of export proceeds which cannot be dealt with
adequately by short-term balance-of-payments support;[41] the International Monetary Fund has a compensatory finance facility in operation for balance-
of-payments support for declines in export earnings
due to commodity price and quantity declines. The
international community, and particularly the United
Nations family of organizations, has much experience
by now in dealing with primary-commodity problems.
The problems are not easily solved, and they obviously are crucial since earnings from these primary
exports, depending on how one defines them, make up
some 80 to 90 per cent of all export earnings of developing countries. But they are at least familiar
problems. Preferences for manufactured goods is a
new issue and its problems and advantages have not
had comparable international examination.

There is another fundamental reason for the
present stress by many developing countries on manufacturing; just as is true for trade relative to
aid, the potential paydirt in growth of export earnings is more promising for manufactures than for
primary products. As can be seen from Table 3, the
rate of growth in industrial production, despite its
slowing down from 1960 to 1964 as compared with 1955
to 1960, has been substantial in the developing coun-
tries--far more substantial than the growth in agriculture,[42] and greater than the rate of industrial
growth in the developed countries.

The United Nations has noted that

> manufactured goods have undoubtedly
> been the most dynamic element in the
> exports of developing countries in
> recent years. Manufactured exports
> from these countries increased during
> 1960-1963 even faster than those of
> fuels; indeed, the rate of increase
> was significantly greater than the

corresponding rate for the developed
market economies or for the world as
a whole.[43]

TABLE 3

Annual Rate of Growth of Industrial Production

(Per Cent)

	1955 to 1960	1960 to 1964
Developing countries	8.1	7.0
Developed countries	4.1	5.6

Source: United Nations, Statistical Office.   Cited
in United Nations Economic and Social Council, World Economic Trends, E/4059, June 29,
1965, Table 8.

Manufactures continue to remain low as a proportion
of total exports of developing countries, as can be
seen from Table 4, but it is just not true that all
developing countries are unable to compete in this
field. Among the developing countries, a very few
dominate in the export of manufactured goods; these
have been, in order of value exported in 1962, Hong
Kong, India, Israel, Mexico, Iran, the Philippines,
Pakistan, Taiwan, Argentina, and Brazil. Among
them in 1962, these ten countries supplied three
fourths of the manufactured exports from developing
to developed countries.[44] This, of course, explains
why particular countries are more interested than
others in the preference issue.

In dealing with the trade gap, so-called, it
should be kept in mind that what the United Nations'
figures referred to was a current-account gap.   The

issue of invisibles, a deficit item, and frequently
a massive one, for most developing countries, is
much on their minds. Issues such as debt service,[45]
maritime costs, tourism, insurance, and patent and
licensing costs, were among the items of concern at
UNCTAD. They are not directly relevant to the preference issue, except as they enter into the gap cal-
culations.

TABLE 4

Percentage of Manufactures[a] in Total Value
of Exports by Developing Countries

	1955	1960	1963
All developing countries	8	9	10
Latin America	3	3	4
Africa	6	6	7
Far East	17	21	25
West Asia	4	5	6

Source: United Nations, Economic and Social Council,
         World Economic Trends, document E/4059,
         June 29, 1965, Table 22, p. 50.

[a]Manufactures include SITC sections 5-8, excluding divisions 67 and 68 but including group 681.

What was intended in this discussion of the gap,
and of the trade fortunes of the less-developed countries in the recent past, was to indicate that the
trade needs of the developing countries for foreign-
exchange purposes are both real and serious, and that
the gap concept has some value in analyzing this

need for particular rather than general cases. What
also emerges is that for most developing countries,
exports of manufactures will not be of any great
consequence for some time to come in their development processes; but for those relatively few countries where they will be important, it is the most
dynamic sector of their export trade and will undoubtedly be the critical element in their future
export performances.

EFFECTS OF PAST PREFERENCE SCHEMES

Before closing this discussion of some of the
underlying concepts and practical considerations mo-
tivating preference proponents, and before moving on
to a discussion of the actual current preference
proposals, a brief note of some existing preference
schemes might be useful.

There is a Commonwealth preference arrangement
in existence. The EEC has its preference arrangements in favor of certain African countries, and
Greece and Turkey. The United States has its preferential trade with the Philippines. Puerto Rico,
which is part of the customs territory of the United
States, thereby enjoys free entry into the United
States. Have these schemes worked to promote the
development of the developing countries involved?
Have preferences fostered trade to the preferred
markets? What lessons might be derived from these
schemes?

The first point to be made is that none of
these arrangements involves preferences by developed
to _all_ less-developed countries generally; and,
thus, none of them is what most developing countries
are now advocating. These existing schemes, therefore, are relevant to the selective or discriminatory preference proposals.

(As an aside to this question, there is a curi-
ous sentence in the paragraph stating the case of the
developing countries in the report of the United

Nations' special committee on preferences which met
in mid-1965. The paragraph makes it clear that "A
general non-discriminatory system of preferences
was favoured because a selective system had various
disadvantages." The paragraph later contains the
following sentence: "The fact that some developed
countries operate a non-discriminatory system of
preferences as among the members of the preferential
areas shows that such a system is not only workable
but also mutually advantageous."[46] What this says,
presumably, is that countries which receive preferences are not discriminated against and that any
system is general as regards these countries. The emphasis supplied on the word "mutually" is to indicate
that the preferences are reciprocal and therefore
also not what the less-developed countries allegedly
are advocating. The cynical conclusion one can draw
from this sentence is that its authors are willing
to stretch the concepts of (a) generalized and
(b) nonreciprocal preferences to whatever extent is
necessary to get some kind of preferences--as long
as their countries are included.)

The accurate answer as to whether existing preference schemes in favor of selected less-developed
countries are serving their stated purpose is that
the evidence is inconclusive.

As regards EEC preferences to the associated
African countries, the preferences, as indicated,
are operative effectively for primary products. One
hears repeatedly from EEC sources that these preferences haven't adversely affected trade of non-
associated less-developed countries, particularly
those in Latin America which export products competitive with those of Africa. The evidence cited
is that Latin American primary-commodity exports to
the EEC have continued to rise substantially despite
the discrimination; and that exports to the EEC of
the associated African countries have not done as
well as Latin America's. The United States Government seems to have accepted this EEC contention.

For example, Assistant Secretary of State
Solomon noted to a congressional committee that

Latin America's exports to the EEC increased by 40 per cent in the five-year period 1959-64, whereas its exports to the world increased by only 17.6 per cent.[47] The State Department has said: "Thus, there is good reason to doubt that preferential entry into the EEC for these products now constitutes any significant advantage for the Africans, and conversely any significant disadvantage to the Latin American countries."[48]

This is an argument that the preferences are useless. The Latin Americans find it hard to agree with this; they assume their trade would be even bigger without the discrimination. Indeed, the Latin Americans must be a bit tired of hearing that discrimination against them doesn't hurt. The logical question to ask is why maintain the discrimination in that case. The African beneficiaries of these preferences believe they have some value. They insisted at UNCTAD, and have since maintained this position, that they will not give up these preferences unless and until they receive equivalent advantages. The relevant paragraph from the UNCTAD resolution on primary commodities reads as follows:

> Preferential arrangements between developed countries and developing countries which involve discrimination against other developing countries and which are essential for the maintenance and growth of the export earnings and for the economic advancement of the less developed countries at present benefiting therefrom, should be abolished pari passu with the effective application of international measures providing at least equivalent advantages for the said countries. These international measures should be introduced gradually in such a way that they become operative before the end of the United Nations Development Decade.[49]

What emerges from an examination of the effectiveness of the EEC preferences to associated African countries is a stalemate: The Latin American countries believe they are hurt by them; the Africans believe they are benefited; the EEC alleges that nobody is hurt, and consequently that no one is benefited, but still will not eliminate the preferences; and the United States has argued that the preferences have no serious effect on Latin America, except in a few cases such as bananas.

Puerto Rican industrial exports to the United States have increased markedly in recent years and these are preferential. But in this case, there is also an important tax incentive for American investment in Puerto Rico, and the trade did not really become significant until the tax incentive became effective.

The Commonwealth countries have in part (Hong Kong, India, and Pakistan, particularly) taken advantage of preferential entry to the United Kingdom market, particularly for textiles; most less-developed Commonwealth countries have not taken very much advantage of the preferences for manufactures. The United Kingdom is the largest importer of manufactured goods from less-developed countries relative to total imports of manufactured goods of any country, but the range of imported goods remains small.[50]

Prebisch noted this point regarding the proportion of the United Kingdom's manufactured imports which come from less-developed countries. He commented:

> Thus, in 1962, so far as total manufactures imported by the EEC countries are concerned, the proportion imported from all developing countries fluctuated between only 1 and 4 per cent, whereas the corresponding proportions were 11 per cent for the United States and 12 per cent for the United Kingdom.[51]

The point made by Prebisch might be amplified for the full year 1963. Table 5 shows the proportion of manufactured imports by various developed countries which came from developing countries.

TABLE 5

Total Imports of Manufactures and Semimanufactures of Selected Developed Countries from All Sources and from Developing Countries, 1963

(Value in millions of dollars; shares in per cent)

Country	Total	From Developing Countries	Share of Developing Countries
United Kingdom	4,389	697	15.9
United States	7,833	1,080	13.8
Japan	1,648	147	8.9
Belg.-Lux.	3,076	200	6.5
West Germany	5,566	352	6.3
France	4,089	189	4.6
Italy	3,583	127	3.5
Sweden	2,249	57	2.5
Canada	4,168	71	1.7
Denmark	1,342	20	1.5
U.S.S.R.	4,796	62	1.3
Netherlands	3,614	45	1.2

Source: State Department research memorandum, RES-9, April 22, 1965. Data from relevant volumes of U.N. Commodity Trade Statistics and IMF Direction of Trade for all countries except the U.S.S.R., and from the Soviet Handbook of External Trade through 1963 for the U.S.S.R. The data cover SITC sections 5-8.

There will be no attempt here to try to explain
why certain countries take a greater or lesser proportion of their manufactured imports from developing countries. There could be many reasons, such as
preferences, the nature of a country's imports, import restrictions of an open or covert nature, and
others. But quite clearly, the reasons are varied
and do not relate only to preferences.

To repeat the essential point: The evidence as
to whether existing preferences, all of which are
selective, are benefiting the preference recipients
--or damaging the countries being discriminated
against--is inconclusive.

One final point might be made regarding existing preferences. Of world exports which move under
preferential tariffs, using the word "preferences"
to include trade among members of free-trade areas
and customs unions as well as other preferences,
about 90 per cent came from developed countries in
1963.[52] Thus while this study deals only with preferences to and among less-developed countries, it
should not be forgotten that developed countries do
benefit from considerable preferential trade--most
of it legalized by the people who wrote the GATT.

SUMMARY

There is no doubt that the less-developed countries as a whole will require considerably more foreign exchange in the future than they have received
or earned to date if they are to continue to make
even modest progress in their growth. It also seems
clear that increased earnings from primary products,
assuming these eventuate, will be insufficient for
this purpose. Greater volumes of aid, some way of
reducing expenditures on invisibles, such as for
debt servicing, and increased exports of manufactures, all must have a role in providing these additional foreign-exchange resources.

The precise amount of this total need is unclear; and as indicated, a total so-called gap

figure may have no relevance for a given country. The United Nations has postulated a total gap on current and capital account of some $11 billion a year by 1970. The IBRD recently suggested a smaller figure for the next several years: "A preliminary study made by the World Bank staff, utilizing available data and their own experienced judgment, suggests that the developing countries could put to constructive use, over the next five years, some $3 to $4 billion more each year than is currently being made available to them."[53]

But whatever the need, individually or collectively, for many of the developing countries some part of it will have to be met by increased exports of manufactured goods.

It is from this starting point that many of the concepts underlying the preference proposals discussed in this chapter are developed. The concepts are important, but they are not really clear or decisive.

"Equality"is not definable, except in the mind of the definer; and simplicity of definition therefore becomes important to compromise the differences among the many definitions. Industrialization undoubtedly will be critical for many developing countries, but whether this should be in light or heavy industry, in the consumer- or producer-goods field, in capital- or labor-intensive activities, will vary country by country--and preference proposals are relevant only to some of these cases. An Indian automobile industry, even if such an industry were desirable on other grounds, would not benefit from tariff preferences into the United States; an Indian toy industry might. Economies of scale, which is one of the basic arguments given in favor of preferences, may or may not exist in many cases. But where such economies do exist, they are likely to be in those industries, such as automobiles for India, where preferences are not now relevant; and economies of scale are likely to be less significant for those industries, such as toy manufacturing in India,

where preferences might help India displace some
other exporter in the United States market.

It is far from clear whether export markets
should precede, be concurrent with, or follow the
development of national markets. It is unclear
whether existing preferences have helped the less-
developed recipients, or hurt the less-developed
countries discriminated against.

In short, while the need for greater foreign-
exchange availabilities by developing countries is
clear; and while the role of greater manufactured
exports by many less-developed countries in meeting
these availabilities is clear; it is not clear that
much of the theoretical underpinning for preferences
made by its proponents is terribly overwhelming.

Notes to Chapter 3

1. Remarks of President Johnson at Howard University, Washington, D.C., June 4, 1965. Release by
the Office of the White House Press Secretary,
June 4, 1965.

2. From Modern Plutarch (Cournos), p. 27, as
given in Stevenson's Home Book of Quotations, p. 1079.

3. The New York Times, August 1, 1965, p. 6,
col. 2.

4. Both citations are from Gunnar Myrdal, An
International Economy, Problems and Prospects (New
York: Harper & Brothers, 1956), p. 291.

5. Harry G. Johnson, "An Economic Theory of
Protectionism, Tariff Bargaining, and the Formation
of Customs Unions," The Journal of Political Economy,
LXXIII, No. 3 (June, 1965), 256-83.

6. C. A. Cooper and B. F. Massell, "Toward a
General Theory of Customs Unions for Developing Coun-
tries," The Journal of Political Economy, LXXIII,
No. 5 (October, 1965), 461-76.

7. A pioneer article in this field is that of Raúl Prebisch, "Commercial Policy in the Underdeveloped Countries," American Economic Review, XLIX (May, 1959), 251-73.

8. Alfred Maizels, Industrial Growth and World Trade: An Empirical Study of Trends in Production, Consumption and Trade in Manufactures from 1899-1959 with a Discussion of Probable Future Trends (New York: Cambridge University Press, 1963), p. 8.

9. Towards a New Trade Policy for Development, Report by the Secretary-General of UNCTAD (New York: United Nations, 1964), p. 20.

10. Final Act of UNCTAD, March 23–June 16, 1964, as reproduced by Her Majesty's Stationery Office, London (Cmnd. 2417), p. 32.

11. UNGA, A/2089(XX). A discussion of the work of the Second Committee of the United Nations leading up to the final resolution on UNOID can be found in A/6191 of December 18, 1965. UNCTAD resolution A.III.1 had recommended the establishment of a specialized agency, rather than an autonomous organization, for industrial development. It is still unclear how the work of the two bodies, UNCTAD and UNOID, will dovetail, and which body will press the hardest for trade preferences for manufactured exports.

12. Towards a New Trade Policy for Development, op. cit., p. 65.

13. For example, this aspect, as well as the dynamics, are treated in the United States submission to the special committee on preferences, UNCTAD documents TD/B/C.2/1/Add.1 and TD/B/AC.1/4/Add.1, June 8, 1965; by Grant L. Reuber, Canada's Interest in the Trade Problems of the Less-Developed Countries (Montreal: Private Planning Association of Canada, 1964); by Harry Johnson in a forthcoming book on U.S. Economic Policy Towards the Less-Developed Countries: A Survey of Major Issues (The

Brookings Institution);and by John Pincus in a forthcoming book for the Council on Foreign Relations.

14. The quoted words are from Prebisch, _Towards
a New Trade Policy for Development_, _op. cit._, p. 23.

15. Annex A.III.3, recommendation adopted without dissent on "Criteria for development of industries with an export potential in developing countries."

16. Annex A.III.8, recommendation adopted without dissent on "Measures and action for the promotion
of trade in manufactures and semi-manufactures among
developing countries."

17. According to _The Economist_ (London), in a
special section on Latin America of September 25,
1965, the Latin American market for passenger cars
is about 300,000 to 400,000 annually, and there are
some 40 Latin American automobile manufacturing
plants (p. xlix).

18. _Ibid_., p. L.

19. Jacob Viner, _The Customs Union Issue_ (New
York: Carnegie Endowment for International Peace,
1950), p. 46.

20. _Ibid_.

21. Gardner Patterson, "Would Tariff Preferences Help Economic Development?" _Lloyds Bank Re-
view_, No. 76 (April, 1965), p. 24.

22. "Nearly one hundred of the developing
countries have each less than 15 million inhabitants
and in two thirds of them the population is less
than 5 million; their national markets are handi-
capped not only by the smallness of their populations but also, in many cases, by their extremely
low incomes per capita" (pp. 22-23).

23. See Charles P. Kindleberger, Foreign Trade and the National Economy (paperback; New Haven: Yale University Press, 1962); K. W. Deutsch and A. Eckstein, "National Industrialization and the Declining Share of the International Economic Sector, 1890–1959," World Politics, No. 13 (1961), pp. 267–99; Simon Kuznets, "Quantitative Aspects of the Economic Growth of Nations: IX. Level and Structure of Foreign Trade: Comparisons for Recent Years," Economic Development and Cultural Change, XIII, No. 1 (October, 1964).

24. For example, see pp. 25–26, and again p. 66.

25. Speech to the American Marketing Association, September 1, 1965, Washington, D.C., Department of State press release No. 202, August 31, 1965. Rostow has developed the national market theme in a great many other speeches.

26. Douglass C. North, The Economic Growth of the United States, 1790–1860 (New York: Prentice-Hall, 1961).

27. Albert O. Hirschman, The Strategy of Economic Development (paperback; New Haven: Yale University Press, 1958).

28. Ragnar Nurkse, Patterns of Trade and Development (Stockholm: Almquist & Wiksell, 1959), pp. 19–20.

29. P. 4.

30. The theme of trade and aid in a qualitative sense is expertly and usefully developed in Johnson's forthcoming book, op. cit., Chap. 2.

31. The detailed discussion of the U.N. technique can be found in the World Economic Survey, 1963, Part I, Chap. 3.

32. Towards a New Trade Policy for Development, op. cit., p. 4.

33. Paragraph 21 of Final Act.

34. Ibid., p. 5.

35. Bela Balassa, Trade Prospects for Developing Countries (Homewood, Illinois: Richard D. Irwin, Inc., 1964).

36. Those of the GATT, the Economic Commission for Europe, and of the United Nations' Department of Economic and Social Affairs discussed above, are summarized in John Pincus, Economic Aid and International Cost Sharing (Santa Monica, California: The RAND Corporation, 1965), Chap. 2.

37. A discussion of this subject can be found in Sidney Weintraub, The Foreign-Exchange Gap of the Developing Countries, Essays in International Finance, Princeton University, September, 1965.

38. The following data are taken from the World Economic Survey, either 1963 or 1964, of the United Nations, and from International Trade 1963 of the GATT.

39. The differences between what the United Nations calls "developing-market economies" and what the GATT calls "nonindustrial areas" is that the latter include Australia, New Zealand, and South Africa, which are considered developed-market economies by the U.N.; and the GATT figures include Yugoslavia among the industrial areas, whereas the U.N. includes Yugoslavia among the centrally planned economies.

40. Pincus, op. cit., Chap. 5.

41. IBRD, Study on Supplementary Financial Measures, requested by UNCTAD 1964, December 6, 1965. This is primarily, but not necessarily exclusively, a question of financing for declines in export earnings from primary commodities.

42. United Nations, Economic and Social Council, World Economic Trends, document E/4059, June 29,

1965. Table 6 shows annual growth rates in agricultural production by region for developing countries, and in no region had these exceeded 2.7 per cent in the period 1959-60 to 1962-63. Referring to the annual growth rate of industrial production between 1960 and 1964 in the developing countries, it is noted that this 7 per cent rate "was substantially larger than the rate of increase in agricultural output in these countries" (p. 20).

43. Ibid., p. 49.

44. United Nations, World Economic Survey, 1963, p. 178. There are some definitional questions whether the countries named should all be considered as developing, but this is an issue which will be discussed subsequently.

45. The most recent thorough discussion of this issue is in Dragoslav Avramovic, et al., Economic Growth and External Debt (Baltimore: The Johns Hopkins Press, 1964). See also Loan Terms, Debt Burden and Development, Agency for International Development, April, 1965.

46. Report of the Special Committee on Preferences, UNCTAD documents TD/B/C.2/1 and TD/B/AC.1/4, June 4, 1965, Paragraph 15.

47. Latin American Development and Western Hemisphere Trade, Hearings before the Subcommittee on Inter-American Trade of the Joint Economic Committee of the Congress, September 8-10, 1965, p. 150.

48. Ibid., p. 197. "These products" refers essentially to coffee.

49. Final Act, Annex A.II.1, "International Commodity Arrangements and Removal of Obstacles and Expansion of Trade," Part II, Paragraph 6. This particular passage was a major achievement of compromise among the developing countries at UNCTAD. They wished to maintain their unity to confront the developed countries and still satisfy the developing

countries receiving preferences as well as those
wishing to get rid of discrimination.

50. The preferential system was studied in
Political and Economic Planning, Commonwealth Pref-
erence in the United Kingdom (London: Allen and
Unwin, 1960).

51. Towards a New Trade Policy for Development,
op. cit., pp. 23-24.

52. State Department estimate made in 1965,
unpublished.

53. George D. Woods, "The Development Decade
in the Balance," Foreign Affairs, XLIV, No. 2 (January, 1966), 214.

CHAPTER **4** GENERAL

PREFERENCES

THERE ARE PREFERENCES AND PREFERENCES

There has been a facile tendency of impartial
outside observers, as well as of partial inside par-
ticipants, to divide the world's countries into two
camps, those in favor of preferences and those
against. At the first UNCTAD, where the developing
countries had the necessary number of votes, this
was the dichotomous way the final resolution on preferences depicted the situation:

> Noting that all the developing countries
> and a great majority of the developed
> countries have signified their agreement
> with the principle of assisting the in-
> dustrial development of developing coun-
> tries by the extension of preferences in
> their favor.
>   Noting, on the other hand, that some
> developed countries participating in the
> United Nations Conference on Trade and
> Development are opposed to this princi-
> ple, and support instead the application
> of the most-favoured-nation principle in
> the extension of concessions by developed
> to developing countries.[1]

Harry Johnson, in a forthcoming book, takes a similar position; he depicts the United States position
(the United States was one of the countries described
in the second quoted paragraph above) as one of near-
isolation in opposition to a sea of preference proponents.[2]

The reality is far more complicated; there are

97

preferences and preferences.[3]   One need only peruse
the report prepared by the Secretary-General of
UNCTAD called <u>Preferences: Review of Discussions</u>,
intended for the use of the special committee on
preferences which met in mid-1965, to get some idea
of the wide disparity of views among the preference
proponents.[4]

The fact that there are more than two positions
was tacitly recognized in the report of the special
committee.[5] This report describes the positions of
countries in favor of general preferences; those in
favor of selective preferences; those in favor of
general preferences based only on the principle of
"competitive need" (which the granting country estab-
lishes); those in favor of nondiscriminatory trade;
and those in favor of general preferences but with
derogations for "the less developed amongst the developing countries." Australia, the United States,
Switzerland, France, Belgium, Israel, the United
Arab Republic, the United Kingdom, the Federal Republic of Germany, and various developing countries collectively, all saw fit to attach annexes to the report to make clear the precise viewpoints of their
governments; and a careful reading of these submis-
sions makes it amply clear that there are profound
differences among preference proponents.

For example, the following are among the reasons
why it is simply inaccurate to define the issue between those in favor and those against preferences:

India favors general preferences and the United
States favors nondiscrimination. Were the United
States to shift its position to one of advocacy of
selective preferences, say in favor of Latin America
and excluding India, quite clearly India would prefer
nondiscrimination over such preferences. The issue
for India is not really preferences or no preferences;
vis-à-vis the United States, it is general preferences or nondiscrimination, even if the Indians have
not phrased it quite that way.

The United Kingdom favors generalized prefer-
ences by <u>all</u> developed to <u>all</u> less-developed coun-

tries. Denmark also does, but with one other major
condition, namely, that Denmark would discriminate
against various developing countries which discriminate against Denmark in favor of other developed
countries. Were the United States to adopt Denmark's
position--and there is considerable logic to this
were the United States ever to move to general pref-
erences--those countries in Africa which give preferences to the EEC, and those in the Commonwealth which
give preferences to the United Kingdom, then would
face discrimination in the United States. These
countries obviously would prefer for the United
States to continue nondiscrimination rather than
adopt a general preference system of this type.

Jamaica likes its present selective preferences
in the United Kingdom. It prefers this situation to
remain, and not for the United Kingdom to join in a
general preference system. This is even more true
for Hong Kong, which probably would be excluded from
the less-developed country ranks in a general system.[6] At some moments Israeli representatives favor
preferences, and at others, probably when the reali-
zation comes that Israel probably would not receive
preferences, they say nothing. The political aspect
of inclusion or exclusion of Israel from the developing country ranks was raised by the United Arab Republic at the meeting of the special committee on
preferences.[7] For Israel, therefore, the position
is not one of being either for or against preferences,
but rather to favor preferences if Israel is included,
and to oppose discreetly if she is excluded. The
African associates of the EEC are in favor of preferences only if they are able to retain some special
position. The French and Belgians both favor selective preferences, but France has indicated it wants
some reciprocity from the less-developed countries
("the negotiation of a preference system should involve the granting of reciprocal concessions. . . ."),[8]
while Belgium does not seem to seek reciprocity ("No
reciprocity would be sought by the party granting the
preference.").[9]

The point being made, and it is an important
one for a policy-maker in any country, is that in

any given case the proponent of nondiscrimination
may be closer to one preference proponent than the
advocates of two different kinds of preferences are
to each other. Ignoring the wheels within wheels on
this question is to misstate the issue from the viewpoint of any realistic policy determination.

   For analytical purposes, there is some merit in
breaking preferences down as between the proponents
of general and selective preferences. The two systems merge at many points, but they diverge drastical-
ly in their conception of the world polity. The
sphere-of-influence,or at least sphere-of-interest,
aspect is never absent in the selective preference
case; or, if not conscious sphere-of-influence, the
idea of favored less-developed country wards is in
the minds of the selective preference proponents.
The general preference proponents, such as the United
Kingdom, Denmark, and many of the larger, more advanced, of the developing countries, have a conception of the world polity in which the general (and
not particular) developed-less-developed country relationship is paramount.[10]

   In the foregoing sense, the general preference
proponents are closer to the conception of global
responsibilities for development propounded in recent years by many United States spokesmen than are
the general and selective preference proponents to
each other.

   As useful as it is to separate general and
special preferences analytically, and politically,
it should be kept in mind that the separation is in
part a false one. It already has been noted that
many less-developed of the developing countries, particularly those already receiving special preferences, want general preferences only if special preferences of some kind also continue. Further, a general system might be extended more widely than to
the country with which it originally was negotiated.
The two systems, therefore, tend to merge. This is
particularly true of a general system with product
derogations, and a system which is selective by
product but in which the product selection begins to

build up. For example, the Japanese have claimed to
favor general preferences to all less-developed countries, but only on a commonly agreed list of products
accepted by all developed countries. This really becomes selective by product. Australia has proposed
and will soon institute a general system, but with
Australia choosing the products on which it will give
preferences, the margin of preference it will give,
and the less-developed countries it wishes to exclude
on the grounds of lack of "competitive need." This
is labeled general, but is close to a selective system, both by product and country. The developing
countries themselves seem to have referred to the
Commonwealth preference system as general as among
its members;[11] any other selective system would be
similarly general among its members.

THE RELEVANT POLICY ISSUES

Most of the remainder of this chapter will deal
with issues relevant to general preference schemes.
The next chapter will deal with the issues related
to selective schemes. Many of the considerations obviously relate to both types; but, for the most part,
it should be self-evident where this is the case and
an effort will be made to avoid repetition.

It already has been noted that some reasons
given in favor of general preferences, and some given
against them, do not seem very substantial. On the
part of those favoring general preferences, for example, it is argued that this is an alternative means
of resource transfer or aid; but this is a useful argument only if the resultant resource transfer is
significant, is better in a technical sense than alternative transfer techniques, or is additional to
existing aid levels. It is in this context that the
aid issue must be discussed; and it will be in the
context of who gets the aid under various systems
that the preference issue must be analyzed.

Another argument given in favor of preferences
is that it is desirable politically, to get the
United States off its isolated hook, so to speak.

This hook is undefined; the political liability is
undefined; and whether getting off a hook at the
moment is really good politics is unclear. The political issue, however, deserves discussion.[12]

One argument cited against preferences is that
they will foster inefficient resource allocation.
This point has been discussed; if anything, it appears that the reverse is the case, that preferences
might actually foster more efficient allocation of
resources, if they would work. It has been argued
that the United States cannot now support preferences, first, because it would require a change in
the law, and secondly, because it is not desirable to
seek this change in the midst of the Kennedy round
of trade negotiations. The first argument is spe-
cious; the Trade Expansion Act will need renewal in
1967 in any event. The second argument has some
validity, but not much; the United States, if it so
desired, could commit itself to seek a change in the
most-favored-nation practice to become effective at
the completion of the Kennedy round.

It has been argued that preferences are too complicated administratively. This depends on the system. Unless the administrative complexity is overwhelming in this era of computers, the argument is
trivial. The argument that for many products no
less-developed country should expect preferences
since they already are more than competitive--for
example, for cotton textiles--also is trivial since,
in such cases, no preferences need be given. The
argument that the United States will be flooded with
cheap imports is also a weak one since safeguards
are possible. The real danger is over-safeguarding,
or the use of quotas as noted below.

The issues which require discussion seem to the
writer to be the following:

1. What are the benefits preferences will give
to developing countries, primarily in a dynamic sense,
secondarily in the static sense of aid transfers?

2. What alternatives might have to be foregone

in seeking a change in United States policy in favor
of preferences? Are the benefits likely to be greater than the costs?

Among the costs which require discussion, in
addition to the level and distribution of aid cited
above, are the following: Will preferences be so
fenced in by quotas (safeguards) that they might do
more dynamic damage than good? Just as it is alleged
there would be some political gain in shifting the
United States position, what would the political
cost be in defining borderline nations as developed?

These seem to be the major potential costs.
They deal with (a) aid, (b) quotas, and (c) definition of countries.

Some other potential costs which should be discussed are: (a) the effect of preferences on future
most-favored-nation tariff reductions; (b) whether preferences are likely to be temporary; and (c) the administrative complexities of certain general systems.

Finally, it is important to analyze the arguments in favor of differentiated preferences based
on degree of development, i.e., to make the degree
of preference inverse to the degree of development,
always keeping in mind that only countries defined
as developing get any preferences in the first place.

There is no one general preference scheme under
international consideration, but a whole host of
them.

Before UNCTAD, Prebisch suggested a system in
which "all developed countries would agree to grant
preferences to all developing countries . . . to be
granted in principle to all imports from the developing countries, subject only to certain specified
exclusions, as well as certain safeguards. . . ."[13]

At UNCTAD, the United Kingdom, in a speech by
Edward Heath, then the Secretary of State for Industry, Trade and Regional Development, advocated general preferences, with three conditions: the need

for all major industrialized countries to "act in
concert"; the consent of Commonwealth governments
whose countries now receive preferences; and the
creation of preferences "not by raising tariffs
against other countries, but by lowering or abolish-
ing tariffs for developing countries."[14] The United
Kingdom later amplified its ideas, stating that any
preferences should be negotiated in the GATT, that
no developed country should be permitted unilaterally to terminate preferences when it felt that the
developing countries' industries were sufficiently
competitive, that the definition of developing countries be tackled in the GATT, and that preferences
should be temporary only in the sense that they
would disappear when most-favored-nation tariff
rates moved to zero.[15]

At the second committee of the first UNCTAD,
which dealt with trade in manufactures, and then
again in a slightly modified form at the special committee on preferences, the developing countries gave
their idea of a scheme. It involved general preferences based on zero duties in developed countries
for some imports from developing countries, and 50
per cent tariff reductions for other products to be
phased down to zero duties within five years. The
scheme envisaged the preferences as temporary, but
for a minimum of ten years and subject to renewal.
The preferences were to be on all manufactures and
semimanufactures, with exclusions justified "in the
appropriate international body," and with safeguards
in the form of tariff quotas (i.e., an in-quota preferential rate and an ex-quota most-favored-nation
rate) to be similarly justified. This "general"
scheme also advocated that "special treatment may be
granted by the developed countries to the less developed amongst developing countries. . . ."[16]

Australia has said it intends to introduce what
it calls a general scheme under which it will give
preferences to countries defined as"less-developed,"
on products and with preferential margins chosen by
Australia, and based on "competitive need" as decided
by Australia.[17] (The United Kingdom had explicitly
rejected the idea of competitive need.) Australia

intends to unilaterally operate its own safeguards.
It is not the purpose of this discussion to analyze
Australia's preference proposal, since it is not the
kind being advocated by most developing countries,
although an examination of it makes it appear minuscule in terms of its potential trade effect and even
more minuscule in terms of its potential impact on
domestic Australian industry. At this writing, the
proposal is under consideration in the GATT, where
Australia has asked for a waiver under Article XXV
of its Article I obligations.

Israel has proposed a general scheme involving
duty-free global tariff quotas to be established by
each developed country in favor of manufactured and
semimanufactured imports collectively from the developing countries more or less collectively. The proposal suggested breaking the developing countries
into two groups, one of more- and one of less-
developed countries, "to permit competition by more
or less equals within the quota limits." The suggested quota was 10 per cent of imports of manufactures and semimanufactures each year (a figure which,
it was noted earlier in Table 5, already is exceeded
by the United Kingdom and the United States).[18]

One other general scheme might be cited, that
suggested by the secretariat of the Economic Commission for Europe some years ago involving preferential
tariff quotas on a country rather than a global basis.
The proposal was the following:

> Each of the industrial countries of west-
> ern Europe might agree, as a realistic
> gesture of immediate aid to the develop-
> ing countries, to abolish all tariffs
> and import restrictions on such exports
> of manufactures by individual under-
> developed countries as do not, in any
> year, exceed a certain proportion--say,
> 3 or 5 per cent--of its total imports in
> the previous year in that commodity
> group. . . . Once they exceeded the
> specified proportion, they would be subject
> to whatever tariffs, or other restrictions

. . . would apply in the absence of the
special preferential treatment proposed
here.[19]

The foregoing by no means exhausts the general
preference proposals extant. Denmark has its variant, which is a liberal one of general preferences
by means of zero duties on most goods to all developing countries except those discriminating against
Denmark in favor of other developed countries. Japan
has its, which is relatively more restrictive than
most other general schemes in its product coverage
since it requires a common list of products on which
preferences would be given by all developed countries. Many academic economists have their own variants. It is not difficult to devise schemes.

The foregoing schemes were given in outline to
indicate how various countries view some of the crucial elements of any preferential scheme. These
crucial elements are the country coverage both of
the givers and receivers of preferences, product
coverage, safeguards, how the safeguards are put into
effect, temporary or permanent, how a temporary preference is terminated, the margin of preference, who
decides this, what is the administering body, how
much unilateral power remains in the hands of the
preference-giver, what about the less developed
among the developing, and similar considerations.[20]

None of the foregoing schemes will be discussed
as such in this study, since details of any proposed
scheme are just that--details, subject to change in
a negotiating context. Instead, the discussion will
focus on the major considerations cited earlier,
which would be relevant to any general preference
scheme in a determination of United States policy.

POTENTIAL BENEFITS OF A GENERAL
PREFERENCE SCHEME

A tariff preference works through the price
mechanism. By affecting returns a less-developed
country can receive from its exports, it might work

in two ways or combinations of the
crease the return to an exporter c
ready being sold abroad; it can r
price sufficiently to permit new
semimanufactured products to be ;
markets. The distinction betwee
significant; it is the distinct:
and dynamic potential of tariff

By focusing on the infant-inu..
advocating preferences, Prebisch was stres......
second alternative above, the dynamic one. By focu..
ing on resource transfers, and the use of preferences as an alternative aid technique, a dynamic element is present, but the stress is really on the
static aspect.[21] Australia's "competitive need"
criterion is an effort to minimize the static, or resource transfer, aspect. The United Kingdom's rejection of "competitive need" as a basis for giving
preferences is an argument that the static and the
dynamic really must be considered together.

The price case for a tariff preference is a
simple one. A tariff raises the price of a commodity to an importer by some amount up to the level of
the tariff. If the tariff then is preferentially removed for the benefit of some exporters--those from
less-developed countries--and not for others, one of
two things can happen for these exporters, keeping
in mind that there should be only one price in the
import market for a given product: Their export
prices can decline by some amount up to the level of
the tariff removed, thus giving the importer some
price advantage; or the exporter's price can rise to
take advantage of the tariff remission, thus benefiting the exporter. The elasticity of demand would be
a big factor in determining the impact on price. A
high elasticity of demand may make price reduction a
paying proposition; a low elasticity may not. For
goods already being exported over the tariff, elimination of the tariff presumably would result in a combination of the two effects, some cheaper price for
the importer, some degree of higher return for the
exporter.

he preferential removal of a tariff would give
referred exporter a potential price advantage
other exporters who would now be discriminated
ainst, but not a <u>preference</u> over domestic producers
in the importing country. (If the tariff was intended
to offset a disadvantage of domestic producers, obviously its elimination, preferentially or otherwise,
will help exporters.) Thus, if a preference is to
work, the competition between preferred exporters
and domestic producers in the importing country obviously is vital. This is why it was argued in an
earlier chapter that talk of preferences to promote
economies of scale in such industries as chemicals
and automobiles in less-developed countries is mostly irrelevant to the preference discussion.

There are, of course, other ways (apart from
greater productivity) to reduce the price of exported
goods, e.g., through subsidies, or exchange-rate
manipulations, including differential exchange rates
(which is a form of subsidy). Many economists have
advocated the export subsidy rather than the preference technique on the grounds that it is less politically complicated. It should be kept in mind, however, that a subsidy has to be financed by the less-
developed country, which is normally poor, while a
tariff preference is financed by the developed country, which is richer. This is the major reason, one
assumes, why the less-developed countries prefer
tariff preferences to subsidies. United States law
calls for countervailing duties against imported
products whose export is subsidized, but in actual
practice the countervailing duty provisions have
rarely been used against less-developed countries,
even when they have resorted to multiple exchange-
rate devices.

Conceptually, the developed country might also
give an import subsidy and thus provide preferred
treatment to developing country exporters even over
domestic producers; as a practical matter this possibility has not yet been advocated forcefully by developing countries.

The price analysis might be carried further.

What actually would happen to the price of an exported
product under a system of tariff preferences?   Since
most manufactured goods are not perfectly competitive,
one assumes there would be a mixture of price shifts.
There might be some price increases by the less-
developed country exporter; there might be some price
shaving by developed country exporters to retain markets; there might be some price shifting by domestic
producers because of the new price structure of the
import trade. The precise primary and secondary
price shifts attendant on new tariff preferences
would require some analysis of demand elasticities
and competitive conditions in the industry on a case-
by-case basis to reach any conclusions. It would
also require some analysis of supply elasticities,
and the extent that production in less-developed
countries could expand to meet any new demand created in the preferred market. Even if there were
perfect supply elasticity, which one doubts would be
the case very often, it is also clear that safeguards on the import side would limit the extent to
which preferences could be used for any single commodity.

Taussig pointed out some time ago that a tariff
preference on existing exports where the preference-
receiving country does not meet all the import needs
of the preference-giving country normally results in
a transfer of funds from the exchequer of the importing country to the exporting producer. "In general,
it may be laid down that any remission of duty which
does not apply to the total importations, but leaves
a considerable amount still coming in under the duty,
puts so much money into the pockets of the foreign
producer."[22] Taussig cited the United States experience with Hawaiian sugar, which he said was precisely
as stated above. Haberler has discussed this same
point of transfers from the exchequer of the importing country to the producer of the exporting country,[23] as has Viner.[24] Viner pointed out that in the
event the preference receiver is unable to supply the
entire market, the preference "will operate virtually
as a subsidy from the treasury of the importing country to the producers in the exporting country"; and
if the preference receiver could supply the entire

market, Viner argued there was no reason not to gen-
eralize the preference to the entire world.[25]

How much money could be transferred this way
from the rich countries to the producers in the poor
countries (who may not themselves be poor, and who
may or may not use the extra receipts for productive
investment)?

One simple static estimate is to take all existing exports of manufactures and semimanufactures
from less- to more-developed countries; assume these
will continue; and assume, further, that all the
tariff receipts foregone by the importing country
will go back to the producer in the exporting country.
The following is a calculation of this type.

TABLE 6

Maximum Price Increases Possible by
Underdeveloped-Country Exporters
on Present Manufactured Exports
from Preferences by
Developed Countries

Exports of manufactures from non-industrial to industrial areas in 1963[a]	$ 3.34	billion
Average ad valorem tariffs on imports of manufactures by the major developed countries[b]	15	per cent
Total import duties which could be foregone (15 per cent of $3.34 billion)	$500	million

Sources:

[a]International Trade, 1963, GATT. It overstates
the trade since it includes exports of such countries as Australia, New Zealand, and South Africa
which surely would not receive preferences.

[b]World Economic Survey, 1963, U.N., p. 185.

The foregoing figure of $500 million, which po-
tentially could have been transferred from the rich
to the poor countries by waiving all import duties
on existing manufactured imports by the former, is
understated because of its static nature. New imports might be created by preferences. But it is
vastly overstated as well, since it assumes that
every last dollar of tariff duty foregone will return to the producers of the less-developed countries, whereas it is likely that importers also
would share in this. It also assumes that the tariff
preferences will cover every manufactured import from
a less-developed country, and that in every case the
preferential rate of entry would be zero. Since textile exports were close to one fourth of the total
export value, and since these are both politically
and economically sensitive in developed countries
and not likely to be subject to preferences, let
alone zero duties, it is quite obvious that the
assumptions overstate the potential transfers.

Some estimates have been made of the potential
increased imports which could result from preferences,
i.e., considering some of the dynamic effects which
might ensue. Reuber has given a figure of some $600
million;[26] Johnson about $1 billion.[27] These esti-
mates make various major assumptions about the nature of the preference system and about demand elasticities; they are short-run estimates. Johnson's
is larger than Reuber's largely because of Johnson's
use of effective as opposed to nominal tariff rates.

None of the estimates, neither the pure resource-
transfer one based on existing exports, nor the estimates combining increased exports with resource transfers but omitting other dynamic elements (particularly new investment and other factors affecting supply),
is of great significance. More comprehensive dynamic
estimates do not exist. As a short-run matter, the
potential gains from preferences are not spectacular.
If there were all gains, and no costs, the preferences would be worth trying since even these relatively small amounts of additional resources of
$0.5 billion to $1 billion are significant; but obviously there would be costs. On the side of import-

ing countries, the total magnitude of potential increased imports from preferences is certainly not
alarming; but this too is relevant to a producer who
would not fear market disruption from imports if there
is assurance that the imports will be spread across
most commodity categories and not concentrated in
his commodity.

The short-run estimates above also are significant in the sense that the benefits would go to a
relatively few countries, those that now are exporting manufactures or have manufacturing facilities in
being. The increased resource transfers, or aid,
would go primarily to India, Mexico, Hong Kong, and
Israel if all were deemed less-developed. Prebisch
has pointed out that these four provide more than
half of the industrial exports from developing countries.[28] Since there is some prospect that all these
areas might not get new preferential benefits, the
benefits would be limited to few countries indeed
over the short run.

In the foregoing discussion assessing the potential benefits of general preferences, one major element was not factored in--the dynamic one of the
foreign private investment which might seek out less-
developed countries to produce for the developed-
country markets. This is essentially an unmeasur-
able, and yet it is critical, just as the whole supply response is. Wage rates, receptivity to foreign
capital, the margin of preference, the fear of quotas
that might go with preferences, the duration of preferences, and similar considerations-- all must be
taken into account in trying to estimate this private
investment factor.

Viewed from the vantage of United States policy,
this foreign investment potential probably is a plus
for preference ideas in the sense that it encourages
private enterprise in developing countries; the work-
ability of the preference idea itself is based on the
market concept and price signals.

However, the attraction of investment probably
would be more concentrated in a system of preferences

selective by country, since attention then would be
focused on investment in that one or few countries
receiving preferences; and it probably would also be
more concentrated in a system of preferences selective by industry, since this would doubly focus attention. This investment attraction may be the
strongest feature of selective plans such as those
advocated by France and Belgium. United States investment in Puerto Rico is based on a selective preference plus a selective tax incentive. Puerto Rico
might not have fared as well if the tax and the preference incentives were both general (and if some of
its people had been unable to emigrate to the United
States).

THE LEVEL OF TARIFF RATES

As was noted above, the maximum price effect of
a preference depends on the tariff rate. The preferential advantage a foreign investor might get also
depends on the tariff rate. Tariff rates are thus a
key to any analysis of preferences. Some relevant
questions are: How high are tariff rates on manufactured goods? Are they high enough to make any difference? What about the Kennedy round? Will granting of preferences build in a vested interest against
future lowering of tariffs?

As was noted earlier, the average ad valorem
tariff rate on manufactured goods in the major developed countries--such as the EEC and the United
States--is around 15 per cent. This is a figure calculated by the United Nations. Calculating "average"
tariff rates is a tricky and, at best, unsatisfactory
operation. It is unclear whether weighted or unweighted averages are better; where the weighting is
by imported value, prohibitive tariff rates are not
counted. Where some rates are very high, as is the
case for the United Kingdom for revenue purposes on
tobacco, the average goes up although there is no
protective intent. A high rate may not be overly
protective; a low rate may be prohibitive. All these
facts are too well known to need repetition, but it
is worth at least citing them in order that the

proper skepticism is put on any average, or on the
alleged precise protective nature of any given rate.[29]

Both the United States Government, in its submission to the special committee on preferences cited
earlier, and Gardner Patterson used this 15 per cent
average to argue that the scope for substantial price
effects from tariff preferences was small. Both
these documents recognized that a 15 per cent average contained some lower rates, where the preferences
truly would be tiny, but also some higher rates where
the preference margin might be significant. But both
argued that the average was a fair approximation of
the total potential of preferences nevertheless.
This has been challenged on several scores.

One challenge is that there are enough high
rates for preferences to be meaningful. The second
and more formidable challenge is that the nominal or
stated tariff rate does not measure the degree of
protection, but that this is done by what has come
to be called in the literature as the "effective"
rates--although this is far too sweeping a word to
use to describe actual protection to any domestic
industry.

What this approach says is that since the tariff
is calculated on the basis of the total imported value
of a product, e.g., 10 per cent ad valorem on the FOB
or CIF value as the case may be; and since both the
foreign and the domestic manufacturers producing the
product in question add only a portion of the total
value; and since the inputs may have borne different
tariff rates from the imported product in question;
therefore, the actual protective effect of a tariff
is different from the stated or nominal rate. For
example, if cotton yarn were dutiable at 10 per cent
ad valorem and the raw cotton from which it was made
dutiable at 0 per cent, and if the production of
yarn involved 50 per cent raw cotton by value and 50
per cent value added--then the effective protection
to a domestic yarn producer would be 10 per cent on
50 per cent, or 20 per cent.

The concept is not new, although it recently

seems to have been rediscovered by economists in
many parts of the world, and considerable work is in
progress measuring effective rates for the major
countries. Viner pointed out that businessmen and
governments "have long known of ways of making increased protection look like movement in a free-
trade direction." He illustrated this: "Removing
the duty on wool while leaving the duty unchanged on
the woolen cloth results in increased protection for
the cloth industry while having no significance for
wool-raising."[30] Clarence L. Barber in Canada and
W. M. Corden in Australia were probably most responsible for bringing the nominal-effective tariff issue
into the current thinking of international trade
economists. In the United States, much useful theoretical and empirical work on this subject has been
done, and is being done, by Harry G. Johnson,
Georgio Basevi, and Bela Balassa.[31] Some of the
points emphasized in these writings is that the disparities between the effective and nominal rates are
particularly significant for simple manufactures produced by developing countries; and that these disparities are compounded by the fact that even the nominal
rates in the tariff structures of most or all countries escalate by degree of processing. This study
will not go into the precise statistical levels of
calculated effective rates, except to note that they
tend to be quite high in the major developed countries (the United States, United Kingdom, EEC, and
Japan) for a wide range of industrial products of
special interest to developing countries.[32]

A good deal of space has been devoted to this
subject of nominal and effective tariff rates both
because the subject is of considerable theoretical
and practical interest in and of itself, and, in
the present context, because preference proponents
have made much of it to show that the potential margins of preference are substantial in many cases.

There is an opposite side to the picture. The
word "effective" tariff rate overstates the case
since the calculation of any effective protection
would have to include much more than is included in
any of the formulae cited above. It would have to

include, for example, subsidies and exchange rate
over- or under-valuations. It also is clear from
the formulae that the less the value added by the developing country exporter, the greater will be the
disparity between the nominal and effective rate.
Thus, a high effective rate may merely indicate a
product of relatively small interest to the exporter.
It has been suggested that countries should negotiate downward the effective tariff rates calculated
in the above manner, rather than the nominal rates.
This type of tariff negotiation would omit the lack
of completeness of the effective rate formula; but
more important, it would permit whopping reductions
in effective rates by granting concessions on those
products for which the exporter adds the least value
rather than on products of greatest export interest.

There is one other major point which must be
considered in the effective-nominal rate discussion.
The products on which the effective rates are highest are usually deliberately chosen. As Viner noted,
protectionists have long known this gimmick even if
theoretical economists have only recently begun to
appreciate it. Thus, for example, some of Basevi's
figures for the United States show effective rates
of between 30 and 80 per cent on textile mill products, about 70 per cent on various leather gloves,
50 per cent on cutlery, and so on. For most of
these products, nominal rates also are higher than
the average. The reason is that these are sensitive
products; and for the most part these are products
in which the developing countries could compete without preferences if they could get reasonable access
to markets. Their importation is restricted by both
high nominal and effective tariffs because this is
the intent. As a practical policy issue, why should
one expect tariffs to be reduced preferentially on
these products on a nonreciprocal basis when countries have been unwilling to do so until now on a
reciprocal basis? What is involved is that many of
these are the kinds of products for which developing
countries rarely need preferences; what they need
are tariff reductions. What the preference issue
has done in part is to endanger the good--that is,
the seeking of most-favored-nation tariff reductions

on products of particular interest to less-developed
countries--by advocating what on the surface seems
better, preferences, but which arouses far more emotional antagonism from producers and workers in the
developed countries.

At this point in time it is hard to predict the
outcome of the Kennedy round. It may significantly
lower industrial country tariffs. If it does, it
will lower both nominal and effective tariffs; and
to the extent it reduces the disparities between the
lower rates for goods at an early stage of processing and the higher rates for goods which have undergone further processing, it will also lower the effective rates more than the nominal ones.

A good case can thus be made that the developing countries should focus not on preferences for
products in which they can compete even without pref-
erences--because they are unlikely to be granted
preferences--but instead should seek to get lower
rates on a most-favored-nation basis; and in particular they should strive to reduce the upward escalation of tariffs as processing and value-added increases.

This relates to some of the earlier discussion
on scale. Most of the industries where the nominal
rates are high, and the effective rates even higher,
those where there is some processing and where the
processed good bears a higher rate of duty than the
good next below it which has undergone one degree
less of processing, are rarely industries where
large-scale production is needed for competition.
Preferences would help for these industries, but so
would lower most-favored-nation rates.

That tariffs do escalate this way is absolutely
clear; and that protectionists knew what they were
doing in bringing about this escalation also is
clear. The GATT has studied this problem[33] as has
the United Nations. Countries which do not grow
their own oilseeds, for example, usually permit the
seed to enter duty-free; the oils are dutiable. The
reason is simple; it is to maintain a domestic oil-

processing industry and the elimination of the oil
duty (and the effective duties clearly are higher
than the nominal ones in such cases) might lead (or
so it is feared) to the elimination of the industry.
In some of these cases preferences would help in
that they would permit selective entry to less-
developed countries but still limit entry to developed countries which may also produce these products.
But in many cases of exorbitant effective rates,
straight tariff reduction of goods which have undergone processing would provide access to developed-
country markets which frequently is now lacking.
Table 7 is reproduced from the World Economic Survey,
1963, to illustrate tariff escalation; the classes of
·manufactures are ranked by their order of importance
in exports from developing to developed countries--
and as can be seen, they generally are products where
duty reduction, and not necessarily only preferences,
are desirable for the developing countries.

TABLE 7

Ad Valorem Tariffs of Selected Developed
Countries on Selected Imports, by Item
and Stage of Processing, 1963
(Per Cent)

Item	EEC	U.K.	U.S.
Cotton			
Raw	0	0	0
Yarn	8	8	14
Woven fabrics	17	18	20
Jute			
Raw	0	0	0
Yarn	10	13	20
Woven fabrics	23	20	6[a]
Leather and leather goods			
Hides and skins, raw	0	0	0
Finished leather	7	13	10
Leather footwear	16	15	13

TABLE 7--Continued

Item	EEC	U.K.	U.S.
Wood			
In the rough and roughly square	0	0	0
Sawn lengthwise	0	0	4
Veneer sheets	10	10	10
Plywood, hardboard, etc.	15	20	25
Iron and steel			
Iron ore	0	0	0
Ingots and other primary forms	7	11	9
Finished articles	9	14	10
Pipes and fittings	14	18	10
Coir			
Raw	0	0	0
Yarn	0	10	0
Woven fabrics	20	20	12

Source: World Economic Survey, 1963, p. 186. Specific duties are converted to ad valorem equiv-
alents. The EEC rates are the common external tariff and the U.K. rates are the most-
favored-nation rates. The U.K. and EEC
tropical timber rates are under suspension.

[a]This is an interesting rate in that it is lower
than the rate for a lesser degree of processing, and
the effective rate may well be negative.

Before closing this discussion of tariffs and
prices, a few words may be useful on the importance
of prices in international trade. Where tariffs,
particularly effective tariffs, are massive, and the
price impact of the tariff therefore can be significant, this obviously is an important trade barrier,

and in some cases a trade bar. But where tariffs, nominal and effective, are more modest, which is the case for the overwhelming majority of tariff items in developed countries, it is far from clear that small price effects have major demand effects in importing countries. The following are quotes from Hansen on this subject: "Prices obviously play a somewhat smaller role in the competitive struggle now than formerly." "All in all in the modern world, price competition is relatively less important than 'marketing competition.'" "Those economists who place great faith in relatively small shifts in the exchange rates probably exaggerate the role of price elasticity."[34]

This point regarding the uncertainty of small price changes is made for a number of reasons. Where tariffs are high, and the price impact might be significant under preferences, this would give less-developed countries a vested interest in maintaining high tariffs. This point will be discussed later. And where tariffs are low, preferences may not be important.

One final point on tariffs evident to all persons familiar with commercial policy: Tariffs count, but not all that much. If the Kennedy round is successful, tariffs will count even less. Given all the nontariff barriers which exist, some overt like quantitative restrictions, some just as pervasive but less obvious such as administrative practices, buy-national policies, over-adjustment at borders for domestic indirect taxes not shifted forward, and given export incentive schemes through direct subsidies, multiple-exchange rates, tax incentives, it is hard to take tariffs in isolation and give too much weight to their precise levels.

The conclusion one might reach from this discussion of tariffs and prices and trade of less-developed countries is that developed-country tariffs do impede trade, but for the most part not significantly; where the tariff barrier is high, and where its elimination would have a significant impact on price, this height is generally deliberate.

The reduction or elimination of such high tariffs is
important--indeed, such tariffs by rich countries
are not fully excusable--and should be pressed by
the developing countries in whatever way is most effective. Given the instinctive reaction in the
United States against giving something for nothing,
and given the tradition of equality and nondiscrimination as the goal, a good case can be made that the
preference route in seeking to reduce duties is
psychologically the wrong one, at least in dealing
with the United States; and that seeking instead to
reduce the escalation of tariffs by degree of processing might be more fruitful.

POTENTIAL COSTS OF GENERAL PREFERENCES

There probably is no great dispute anywhere any
more about the overwhelming need for development by
the less-developed countries; or in the proposition
that whatever else is needed for development, some
industrialization and some degree of capital imports
are essential for most less-developed countries; or
in the understanding that both trade and aid have
their roles in the amassing of foreign exchange by
less-developed countries for their necessary imports.
These all are taken as given here.

Gunnar Myrdal has eloquently and forcefully
stated the development case over and over again. He
has contended that preferential advantages to the
underdeveloped countries, if they helped in this development process, would be "in line with American
ideals of liberty and equality. . . ."[35] Prebisch
has vigorously stated the case for preferences.

If all that were involved were benefits from
preferences, no matter how small the benefits, there
would be little purpose in discussing the issue.
But it is the subject of international discussion,
and of this study, because it is not that simple.
While preferences are not all the same, all have
costs. The costs might be in choices foregone, such
as the alternative noted above with respect to altering tariff structures in developed countries; and

they could be in the price the developing countries
would have to pay for preferences, which was the
essential reason George Washington abjured the
search for preferences on the part of the young
United States.

In the United States, which is the focus of
this study, some informed and well-argued effort has
to be made to indicate the policy consequences of seeking a change from nondiscriminatory to discriminatory
treatment of developing countries. In another context, Haberler has made the following comment:

> The policy of speeding a country's de-
> velopment through customs protection
> or other measures is a task of great
> difficulty and complexity. Recommend-
> ing and evaluating such a policy, to
> say nothing of carrying it through, re-
> quires a good deal more than keen theo-
> retical analysis. What is also needed
> is a vast factual knowledge, good judg-
> ment, and above all, a sense for histori-
> cal, political, and social development
> concerning the practical-political feasi-
> bility of a rational policy of protec-
> tion.[36]

The same comment could be made about recommending, evaluating, and carrying out a preference policy.

Potential costs of general preferences which
have been cited by responsible analysts, and which
seem to have some degree of validity, will be set
forth. This is not to say that these costs, singly
or collectively, necessarily outweigh the potential
benefits of preferences. They may. But the essential reason for outlining these costs is so that
they will be considered. If the costs are deemed
too high, general preferences should be rejected; if
general preferences ever are adopted despite the
potential costs, the system can at least be devised
to minimize the dangers involved. This last point
will be treated in the concluding section of this
chapter.

Over-Safeguarding

To anyone reading the United States submission
to the special committee on preferences, it is evident that the policy-makers were fearful that preferences, instead of liberalizing world trade, would
lead to new trade restrictions:

> There is a good basis for arguing that
> tariff preferences would not signifi-
> cantly help to increase exports of manu-
> factured and semi-manufactured goods of
> developing countries generally. And,
> surprisingly, however, at the same time,
> all admit that there is need for special
> safeguard measures to protect against
> potential market disruption. The result
> of this fear of market disruption could
> be the imposition of new import restric-
> tions ostensibly required because of
> tariff preferences and aimed primarily
> at the export-oriented industries of
> the developing countries.[37]

Patterson has made this same point:

> Once such a major departure from most-
> favoured-nation treatment and traditional
> liberal trade doctrine had been sanc-
> tioned, must we not anticipate that
> Congress would insist on granting "pref-
> erential" treatment, probably in the
> form of non-tariff safeguards, to many
> domestic producers who also are not
> competitive with foreign producers?[38]

This feeling, that if the United States gave unrequited preferences it also would insist on the
unilateral right to impose any necessary safeguards,
obviously cannot be documented beyond dispute, but
there is some strong evidence supporting it. The
kinds of industries in developing countries that
would most likely benefit immediately from preferences would be labor-intensive; and to the extent
the preferences were successful, they would hit

hardest at the outset at the industries already in
most trouble in developed countries. It would be
one thing to let these declining industries in developed countries adjust over time to what might be
considered "normal" competition; it would be hard
politically to resist safeguarding these industries
from preferential trade.[39]

        There is some experience to buttress this fear.
The United States-Philippine Trade Agreement of 1955
contains provision for quotas on a most-favored-
nation basis, but even more significantly, it permits discriminatory quotas if investigation reveals
that "as the result of preferential treatment accorded pursuant to this Agreement, any article of
the other country is being imported in such increased
quantities and under such conditions as to cause or
threaten serious injury to domestic producers of like
or directly competitive articles." The Agreement
continues that any action taken pursuant to the foregoing sentence should be the subject of consultation
before the action is taken, but: "It is understood
that this right of consultation does not imply that
the consent of the other country to the establishment of the quota is needed in order for the quota
to be put into effect."[40]

        The foregoing is a unilateral right to put quo-
tas into effect. Australia, under its concept of
"competitive need," also wishes to maintain the unilateral right to discriminate against any less-
developed country it feels no longer needs the preference. This can be another form of over-safeguarding
against efficient exporters among the developing countries. It also institutes a peculiar kind of trade
incentive; as soon as a less-developed country is
competitive in a given product, it must prepare itself to face discrimination since it must then face
a most-favored-nation tariff while other less-
developed countries are given preferred treatment.

        The developing countries have recognized that
safeguard clauses would be needed under any preferential system, but their proposals would have some international body, in which they would have the

majority vote, control these safeguards. It is hard
to see the United States, if it were to give unrequited preferences, also giving away its unilateral
right to protect itself.

There is a certain anomaly in this argument
about quotas, one which is apparent in the United
States submission to the special committee on preferences cited above, namely, even if preferences won't
help much, that severe safeguards against injury
still would be needed. Prebisch pointed to the ex-
aggerated fears in the developed countries of market
disruption from manufactured imports from the underdeveloped countries:

> The magnitude of this problem is often
> exaggerated. Actually, exports of manu-
> factures from the developing countries
> amounted to somewhat in excess of $2
> billion in 1961 and, even assuming an
> increase of $10 billion by 1970, i.e.,
> by more than half the trade gap, this
> would represent only some 4-5 per cent of
> the total increment in the consumption of
> manufactures calculated for the developed
> countries from 1961 to 1970.[41]

But the assurances are not good enough. Even
if Prebisch's global figures are correct, this would
not mollify the workers and owners in industries affected. One would think the shoe industry, to name
only one, would gladly give preferences if at the
same time a global import quota were instituted.
There is an anomaly. Even if preferences were not
of much help, this would not prevent Congress, were
it to grant authority for preferences, from writing into the same legislation unilateral safeguard
measures. And once written into the legislation,
the great danger is that the safeguards would be
used.

The United States has not resorted to many absolute quotas for manufactured goods, despite alleged
market disruption, but this liberalism has been maintained in the context of reciprocity and the most-

favored-nation clause. The ground rules would be
different under a nonreciprocal preferential regime.

The foregoing is judgmental. It could be inaccurate. But there is no doubt that many of those
most experienced with United States commercial policy, many of the same people who have been in the
forefront in promoting a liberal trade policy for
the United States, have reached the judgment that
one price that would have to be paid to get a change
in the law to permit preferences would be a reversion
to quotas and protectionism. And if this were an accurate judgment, the quotas would affect precisely
those industries in which the less-developed countries were most competitive. The price could be a
high one.

Aid Distribution

The perennial issue of trade versus aid keeps
coming up with respect to the preference issue.
Preferences are a form of aid. Hansen says he likes
preferences because they are aid "through normal economic processes."[42] Johnson's forthcoming book dis-
cusses whether aid through aid or aid through trade
is better, and in general he opts for aid through
trade. Patterson raises the question of how much
aid can be provided by preferences.[43] Call it what
one wishes, the static aspects of preferences, the
ability to permit producers in less-developed countries to raise prices on products they already are
selling, is pure aid.

The hope, obviously, is not only that preferences might be better than other forms of aid, but
that they should also be additional. As the submission of the less-developed countries to the special
committee on preferences put it: "The developed
countries granting the preferential treatment described above shall not nullify or impair the positive effects of preferences . . . by reducing their
aid to the developing countries. . . ."[44]

There seems to be a good deal of naiveté in all

this. There is no doubt in the mind of the author
that existing aid levels, and terms and conditions
of aid, must be improved, and improved substantially.
But it can hardly be expected that aid through trade
preferences will be lost in the shuffle because it
is more camouflaged than aid through aid channels.
One need only examine United States Congressional
hearings on past preferential arrangements; they
were thought of as being in lieu of some amount of
aid in the development process.[45] In the European
Common Market discussion of its association arrangements with Greece, Turkey, and the eighteen African
states, the trade preferences afforded these countries clearly were intended in part as a tradeoff
for some amount of other forms of aid. It would be
unrealistic to expect parliaments to give aid in
this form, and then ignore this aid in its consideration of the total aid appropriation.

This point is germane not because preferences
are an inferior form of aid--they may be, but there
is considerable evidence that they are not--but only
because they are some form of aid and will affect
the total. It is a form of aid that will go primarily to a few countries, those able to export the manufactured products on which preferences are given, and
thus affect the distribution of aid to all countries.
Given the present state of their export trade, it
would be a good form of aid to, say, India and
Mexico; it would be less good for, say, Nigeria and
Chile.

This is not an argument against preferences,
but it is an important consideration, a possible
price, that should not be ignored.

The Definition of Countries

The definition of countries for preference purposes may seem simple in the abstract but is not
really an easy issue for people concerned with political and economic relations with other countries.
The United States submission to the special committee
on preferences took this point into account. It

raised the point whether

> for example, Hong Kong, Taiwan, Israel,
> Kuwait, Ireland, Iceland, Finland,
> Turkey, Greece, Spain, Portugal, Mexico,
> Venezuela, Argentina, Yugoslavia, and
> other centrally-planned economies [would]
> all be expected to receive preferences.
> Would they be expected to grant prefer-
> ences to others?[46]

Prebisch recognized that there is a "small group of borderline cases at the top of the per capita income range and it is not an easy matter to establish the cut-off point among them."[47]

There are other areas in which the problem arises whether to define a country as developed or less-developed, e.g., for procurement purposes under the United States aid program, or under the United States interest equalization tax, or in the United Nations itself for the Special Fund or for financing under the emergency operation in the Congo which had a lower scale of assessments for less-developed coun- tries, or with respect to Part I and Part II coun- tries under the International Development Associa- tion. But these really are not of the same genre as trade preferences; a country not eligible for pro- curement under the United States aid program, to take one example, loses a marginal privilege. But a country declared ineligible for trade preferences not only loses a marginal privilege, but must face active discrimination against its manufactured ex- ports to developed countries. As businessmen in borderline countries lose sales because of discrim- ination, this becomes a political as well as eco- nomic issue.

Presumably no one would ask a borderline coun- try to give preferences, but in a two-classification world, a country which is not less-developed is ipso facto developed.

There really are no automatic criteria which will solve the problem. The developing countries

have argued that Hong Kong should not be considered
as one of them for preference purposes. Hong Kong's
per capita income in 1962 according to United Nations
statistics was about $360; Venezuela, Argentina,
Chile, Panama, Lebanon, Costa Rica, and several
other countries which certainly would consider themselves less-developed had higher incomes. With respect to value added in manufacturing on a per capita
basis, Mexico, Venezuela, Argentina, Uruguay, Yugoslavia, just to name a few, ranked higher than Greece
or Turkey.[48] On the share of manufacturing in the
gross domestic product, Argentina and Chile, to name
just two, rank higher than Turkey.[49] Composite in-
dexes could be compiled, but any country omitted
would be unsatisfied with the elements entering into
this index and could easily suggest alternatives.

     The point need not be labored; but clearly,
this is not an economic decision alone. Any developed
country granting preferences would have to decide for
itself the political costs of excluding some other
country from the benefits, or the political gains of
including it. Politics being a matter of self-
interest, the benefits might be turned on and off,
as aid and diplomatic relations sometimes are.
Political relations being what they are, no one
would really expect the United States to grant preferences to less-developed Communist countries unless
there were some major political considerations at
stake, if even then.

     Probably the only way for a country like the
United States to solve the definition issue and not
alienate too many countries were it to grant preferences would be to give preferences to everybody,
underdeveloped or borderline, although God only
knows where that borderline is; and then hope for
the best that the preferences won't be turned on and
off too frequently for political purposes. (The definition problem is easier but not absent under a
selective system, since whenever a country wished to
give a preference, the preference recipient is by
the giver's definition less-developed.)

     Even if there were some political disability in

advocating a nondiscriminatory world trading system, which some have alleged is the case for the United States, the obverse clearly is not true; there is no great political gain to be made from giving preferences.[50] What "gain" there is, would be a momentary bit of popularity in some international forum. The popularity would wear off, and indeed the disillusion would set in, if preferences, once given, did not work too well. Giving preferences would not be the end of the popularity picture; it would barely be the beginning. There would not seem to be much of a political case for preferences unless the economic case is overwhelming; and, in that event, preferences are their own justification.

Future Tariff Reductions; Duration
of Preferences

Most proponents of preferences claim that preferences would be needed only as a temporary device and could be terminated once they have served their purpose. It also has been argued that preferences would not deter future most-favored-nation tariff reductions since every country, particularly a developed country, has it in its own power to reduce its own tariffs. This is a weak argument since it merely states that any country can unilaterally lower its own tariff; it says nothing about reductions by other developed countries in favor of one's exports. There are numerous precedents of developed countries refusing to lower tariffs in favor of third countries in order to maintain a preference given to privileged trading partners.

Prebisch made much of the temporariness of preferences: "Since the new preferential system is intended as an encouragement to infant industries, it will be evident that some provision must be made for the elimination of preferences once the industries are firmly established."[51] Prebisch had some elaborate ideas of the staggering of commencement and termination of preferences by country and industry as new industries (companies?) formed, so that even this temporariness of preferences would be around for a

good many scores of years. The developing countries
in their own suggestions were a bit more vague about
the word "temporary"; instead they talked of preferences for "at least ten years," subject to renewal
by five-year stretches.[52]

As a political matter, can one really expect
that "temporary" preferences, once given, will later
be removed? Is there really anything more permanent
than this kind of temporary treatment where vested
interests get built in? The United Kingdom recognized this. It argued that once preferential rates
were reduced to zero, the temporariness of preferences should be achieved by most-favored-nation
rates moving to zero, not by trying to raise the
preferential rates. Given the imperial preference
system, this is an area in which the United Kingdom
has had some experience.

The United Kingdom position leads one naturally to
ask whether preferences, once given, might also lead
to vested interests and pressure by developing countries benefiting from them to maintain the most-
favored-nation rates high so that the margins of
preference will remain meaningful. This is an important point, perhaps more so for selective than for
general preferences where the benefits are more diffuse and the pressure consequently also more diffuse;
but even under general preferences there will be primary beneficiaries among the less-developed countries
in the case of any particular product. If giving
preferences will materially diminish the probability
for reducing tariffs among the world's major trading
countries, the price of preferences must then be considered too high. This is a danger which concerns
commercial policy officials, and not without some
reason.

One major reason is that tariffs and other
trade restrictions have been and are being maintained for the purpose of permitting preferences.
This is certainly the major reason for the EEC tariffs on coffee, cocoa, bananas, and other tropical
products--the tariff permits preferences to associated African producers. If revenue were the purpose

of the tariff, there would be no reason to forgive
the tariff for the African associates. And for tea,
which is not of primary interest to the African associates, the EEC suspended all tariffs on imports
from all sources. The United Kingdom retains formidable restrictions against United States citrus, despite trade-agreement commitments to the contrary,
for the purpose of giving preferences to Jamaica and
Trinidad and Tobago. The United States in past trade
negotiations has had to negotiate, by giving reciprocal tariff concessions of its own, to reduce various
Commonwealth preferences. In other words, there is
much experience to show that the existence of preferences has acted as a bar--in a few cases, an insur-
mountable one--to most-favored-nation tariff reductions. As noted earlier, this consideration, while
present under general preferences, is even more important to selective preferences.

The French, with impeccable logic, have made
this point explicit. In a paper prepared for UNCTAD,
it was pointed out that since developed countries
cannot really subsidize manufactured imports from
developing countries because of the budgetary problem involved, therefore: "In practice, this means
that the industrialized countries would have to maintain or impose custom duties of such a nature that
exemption therefrom of imports from the developing
countries would make such imports possible."[53]   Or
again: "Thus for example, a measure calling for the
abolition of duty on a particular product is not compatible with another measure providing for a preferential tariff on the same product."[54]

Administrative Problems

At an earlier point in this chapter, an ECE secretariat proposal was cited,calling for tariff preferences by particular developed countries in favor
of less-developed countries on an item-by-item basis,
by means of tariff quotas (i.e., an in-quota preferential rate and an ex-quota most-favored-nation
rate). The value of this genre of proposal is that
it would give an opportunity for preferential trade

to the less-developed of the developing countries by
not permitting the more developed to preempt the entire preferential quota. This would be a complicated
system. If one took 20 developed countries and 80
less-developed countries and only 100 tariff items,
this would give 160,000 tariff quotas. This kind of
arithmetic will be just as relevant under various
selective preference schemes.

Thus, even though complexity of administration
should not necessarily be a bar to preferences, it
is a consideration if the system would be a monster.
A good general rule, probably, is that all other
things being equal, simplicity is desirable. One of
the great virtues of the most-favored-nation system
is its simplicity; the burden of proof for changing
this into administrative chaos, which could be true
under certain preferential systems, rests on those
who allege that possible chaos notwithstanding, the
new system is better.

The arguments in favor of differentiated preferences by degree of development are also subject to
criticism on the grounds of administrative complexity. (This is in addition to the argument of
Prebisch, that tariffs might not be high enough to
have meaningful gradations of preferences.)

CONCLUDING COMMENTS ON GENERAL PREFERENCES

Pressures on the United States to shift its
policy--to adopt a system of general preferences--
can be expected to continue. Primarily this is because the United States is the key country if a general preference system is ever to become a reality.

One suspects that another reason one should expect these pressures to continue is because spokesmen from less-developed countries sometimes believe
that with persistent pressure, the United States has
a tendency to alter its policy. Prebisch has him-
self personally witnessed a reversal of United States
policy from refusal even to talk about commodity
agreements to taking the lead in bringing about the

coffee agreement. At the second session of the prep-
aratory committee for UNCTAD, the Brazilian delegate,
Jayme Rodrigues, made a long speech arguing that the
United States eventually supported the Inter-American
Development Bank, various aspects of the Alliance for
Progress, and the desirability of economic planning, but
only after "stubborn persistence on the part of the
Brazilian representative. . . ."[55]

A much more meaningful form of pressure on the
United States to alter its stance from a policy viewpoint, however, is the potential proliferation of systems of selective preferences in the world despite United
States opposition. As noted, in part this proliferation is taking place in the form of new EEC association arrangements with Nigeria and possibly other
countries in Africa, such as Kenya, Tanzania, Uganda,
and particularly the Maghreb countries. It is possible that the EEC will seek certain selective preferences in other parts of the world, such as Latin
America. Australia plans to institute its preference system.

It may turn out that the United States, in self-
protection, will decide to join the pro-preference
countries. This joining might take the form of
selective preferences, particularly of a regional
nature with Latin America. This will be discussed
in the next chapter. However, if it should turn out
that the United States should wish, as a defensive
step, to adopt some preference system, the following
general preference ideas are suggested. These are
designed to minimize potential costs of general preferences of the type discussed above.

For example, the United States might adopt certain aspects of the United Kingdom proposal and make
zero duties the goal in international trade for industrial goods. In the United Kingdom proposal,
this is only a pious hope. The United States might
suggest that preferences to all less-developed countries be given only after a tariff negotiation in
which the major developed countries agreed to move
most industrial tariffs to zero, staged over, say,
ten to fifteen years. This is an argument for

something close to free trade, a subject already
amply discussed in the literature.

This would give temporary and degressive preferences to the less-developed countries as the most-
favored-nation rates came down to zero.   It would
solve the problem of making preferences temporary; and
it would assure that most-favored-nation rates would
not be kept high to maintain preference margins.   It
would ease the definition problem since the definition would be crucial only for a temporary period;
and even during that period the discrimination would
be declining progressively.   It would eliminate the
problem of tariff escalation by degree of processing.
This would not be an administratively complex system,
and it would not do permanent violence to the rationale underlying the most-favored-nation principle.
From an economic efficiency viewpoint, at this point
in history the developed countries certainly would
benefit.   It would not prevent the less-developed
countries from using tariffs of their own for their
own development purposes.

The idea of free trade among industrial countries for a wide range of industrial goods is not
revolutionary.   The 80 per cent clause of the Trade
Expansion Act of 1962, which permitted negotiation
for zero duties for those categories in which the
United States and the EEC together accounted for 80
per cent or more of aggregated world exports, came
to naught because of the failure of the United Kingdom application for membership in the EEC, but this
legislation permits a major step to free trade in industrial goods.[56]   The kind of free-trade proposal
suggested here obviously would contain exceptions
and safeguards and provision for assistance to affected industries and workers.   But it would minimize the danger of quotas accompanying preferences as
an over-safeguarding   device since it would not
give unrequited benefits, but be in the context of a
reciprocal negotiation.   It similarly would ease the
aid aspects of preferences since the zero duties and
temporary preferences to less-developed countries
would be in the context of a quid-pro-quo negotiation with other developed countries.

From an economic viewpoint, this is an initiative which makes sense. Practically, its feasibility is marginal, if even this good. It would require approval by the United States Congress, and this is doubtful, although quiet tests might be made. It would require agreement by the other key industrial countries (particularly the EEC and EFTA countries, and Japan), and this, too, is doubtful. But it, too, may be worth a try.

The United States might also adopt certain Danish ideas, i.e., to give preferences to all countries defined as developing except those that discriminate against the United States by giving preferences to other developed countries. This would mean no preferences for various Commonwealth developing countries such as India which now give preferences to the United Kingdom, or for African associates of the EEC--until the United States achieved equality of treatment in these developing-country markets. The purpose of this suggestion is to strike an important blow for the open-door principle. It would also assist the developing countries concerned by permitting them to buy in the cheapest markets. This idea could be married with the previous one of coupling preferences with a commitment among developed countries to move to zero tariffs on manufactured goods.

If the United States ever adopted general preferences, and if a developed-country-zero-duty scheme of the foregoing type did not succeed, the United States almost certainly would adopt certain aspects of the Australian model; namely, deciding unilaterally: the products on which preferences should be given; what safeguards should be used and when; what countries should be defined as "less-developed"; what margin of preference should be granted; when a preference should terminate. This would almost certainly be a necessary concomitant of unilateral, unrequited preferences; it also would be a form of trade anarchy, if adopted by many developed countries, each acting on its own. It would not make for a harmonious trading world.

The foregoing suggestions (zero duties and open
door) are given not because they are necessarily
practical, but rather because they seem more desirable than other general preference proposals extant.
The zero-duty suggestion would, of course, lead to
a nonpreferential world over a given time period.

All the comments made about the potential costs
of preferences deal with the implementation of general preference proposals at this time in history.
At some future time, the cost calculation might differ. By the same token, particularly if there should
be a successful and substantial lowering of tariffs,
the potential benefits might differ from those estimated now.

But, with this limitation that the benefit-cost
discussion deals with the present, one can't help
but get the feeling that, except for a few countries,
there is much ado about very little advantage in
most general preference ideas.

In remarks during the second session of the
Trade and Development Board created by UNCTAD, Prebisch voiced some disquiet that a preference war
might start, i.e., different countries might adopt
different systems. Some years ago, Haberler made
much the same point:

> It is of especial and vital importance
> for small countries that the world
> should keep, at least in principle,
> to this policy [i.e., most-favored-
> nation policy]. If a short-sighted
> policy of discriminating treatment
> came into fashion, the small and weak
> countries, who cannot offer such im-
> portant economic concessions as the
> large ones and who have not sufficient
> political influence to prevent others
> from discriminating against them,
> would suffer heavy loss.[57]

This point is more germane to selective, negotiated
preferences than to general ones, but, as indicated

earlier, the two have many points in common. A certain sense of anarchy may be inevitable as one con-
templates: quotas; tariff quotas; definition of
countries; differentiation of degree of preferences;
staging of preferences and phasing some in and phasing others out as no longer needed; fighting against
vested interests that wish to keep most-favored-
nation rates high in order to keep preferences somewhat significant; and the other paraphernalia that
almost inevitably must accompany a departure from
the simple definition of what is "equal treatment."

And if the potential gains are limited in scope
and to a few nations, one wonders whether the price
may not be too high. If it is true that the benefits
to developing countries generally might be just or
almost as great from most-favored-nation reduction
in tariff rates by stage of processing, without the
costs, one also wonders whether the developing countries have chosen the right tactic.

Most-favored-nation reductions in tariffs on
goods at later stages in the manufacturing process
would, if achieved, be obtained by developing countries as a matter of right, not of charity. Unrequited preferences, if granted, must inevitably be
in the nature of a privilege granted, a form of
noblesse oblige, and this kind of patronizing seems
less satisfactory in today's world. And the charity
giver must inevitably call the tune.

The conclusion reached here is that a system of
general preferences of a type that might be generally beneficial, involving zero import duties by developed countries for most manufactured goods within
a reasonable time period, is worth testing quietly
but is probably not now feasible; and that other
general preference systems are not now desirable.

Notes to Chapter 4

1. UNCTAD, Geneva, March 23-June 16, 1964,
Final Act, Annex A.III.5.

2. Harry G. Johnson, U.S. Economic Policy
Towards the Less Developed Countries: A Survey of
Major Issues (Washington, D. C.: The Brookings In-
stitution), forthcoming.

3. Some hint of this reality is given in a report written shortly after UNCTAD by Frederick
Strauss, U.S. Department of Commerce, called simply
"Report on UNCTAD" July, 1964. The full report was
unpublished, although extracts appeared in International Commerce Weekly.

4. UNCTAD document TD/B/AC.1/1 and Corr. 1,
March 23, 1965.

5. TD/B/C.2/1 and TD/B/AC.1/4, June 4, 1965.

6. Indeed, at UNCTAD, Hong Kong representatives
quietly but persistently urged the United States representatives to stick to their guns in favor of nondiscrimination.

7. TD/B/C.2/1 and TD/B/AC.1/4, June 4, 1965,
annexes B.5, and addendum 1 and addendum 2 to this.

8. Ibid., Annex B.3.

9. Ibid., Annex B.6.

10. One of the stories making the rounds at
UNCTAD was that the United Kingdom favored general
preferences deliberately to shuck its special relationships with such countries as India and Pakistan
in the trade field. The United Kingdom is now the
world's most important developed-country importer of
manufactured goods from developing countries under
preferential regimes, and a general preference system
would enable the United Kingdom to share these preferential imports with other developed countries.

11.   In the report of the special committee on preferences.

12.   The basic case made in favor of preferences in Harry Johnson's book, op. cit., is a political one, although all the supporting discussion is essentially economic.

13.   Towards a New Trade Policy for Development, report by the Secretary-General of UNCTAD, New York, 1964, pp. 68-69.

14.   UNCTAD, Geneva, March 23-June 16, 1964, Final Act with Related Documents (London: Her Majesty's Stationery Office, 1964, Cmnd. 2417).

15.   TD/B/C.2/1/Add.1 and TD/B/AC.1/4/Add. 1, June 8, 1965, Annex B.8.

16.   Ibid., Annex B.4.

17.   Ibid., Annex B.1.

18.   Ibid., Annex B.5.

19.   Economic Survey of Europe in 1960, prepared by the Secretariat of the Economic Commission for Europe, Geneva, 1961, p. 50.   (E/ECE/419.)

20.   These are discussed in the UNCTAD document cited above, Preferences: Review of Discussions, TD/B/AC.1/1 and Corr. 1.

21.   Gardner Patterson's article, "Would Tariff Preferences Help Economic Development? " Lloyds Bank Review, No. 76 (April, 1965), pp. 18-30, deals more with the static than the dynamic element.   So, too, does the United States submission to the special committee on preferences, TD/B/C.2/1/Add.1 and TD/B/AC.1/4/Add.1, Annex B.2

22.   Frank William Taussig, "Reciprocity," Quarterly Journal of Economics (October, 1892).   Reprinted in Free Trade and Tariff Reciprocity (New York: Macmillan, 1920), pp. 120-33.   Quoted sentence is from p. 122.

23. Gottfried von Haberler, The Theory of International Trade (New York: Macmillan, 1936).

24. Jacob Viner, "The Most-Favored-Nation Clause in American Commercial Treaties," The Journal of Political Economy, XXXII, No. 1 (February, 1924), 101-29.

25. Ibid., pp. 105-06. In an unpublished comment, undated but written in 1964, Jaroslav Vanek has pointed out that there would be a tendency for less-developed countries to ship their manufactured products to the markets in which domestic prices were highest, normally the countries where tariffs were highest and the margins of preference greatest, since their returns would then be greatest. He has noted that (except for limitations due to transportation costs, lack of homogeneity of manufactured products, and quotas in developed countries) there might also be a tendency for developing countries to ship their own manufactured products to the highest tariff market and in turn import the similar product back from developed countries.

26. Grant Reuber, Canada's Interest in the Trade Problems of the Less-Developed Countries (Montreal: Private Planning Association of Canada, 1964), pp. 23-29.

27. Johnson, op. cit.

28. Towards a New Trade Policy for Development, op. cit., p. 24, footnote.

29. Randall Hinshaw, The European Community and American Trade, published for the Council on Foreign Relations (paperback; New York: Frederick A. Praeger, 1964), contains some excellent summaries of tariff rates in various Atlantic community countries and country-groupings. The studies, some weighted, some unweighted, are those of the U.S. Committee for Economic Development, the U.K. Political and Economic Planning, a Swiss study for 1955, a GATT study of 1952 and a more recent EEC study. Bela Balassa, "Tariff Protection in Industrial Countries: An

Evaluation," The Journal of Political Economy, LXXIII,
No. 6 (December, 1965), 573-74, is a more recent attempt at measuring comparative tariff rates, using
both nominal and effective rate ideas.

30.   Jacob Viner, The Customs Union Issue (New
York: Carnegie Endowment for International Peace,
1950), p. 48.

31.   Many of the studies are still forthcoming
as this is written. Some of the material which has
appeared is Harry G. Johnson, "The Theory of Tariff
Structure, with Special Reference to Trade and De-
velopment," in Johnson and Peter B. Kenen, Trade and
Development (Geneva: Librairie Droz, 1965), pp.
9-29; Clarence L. Barber, "Canadian Tariff Policy,"
Canadian Journal of Economics and Political Science,
XXI, No. 4 (November, 1955), 513-30; W. M. Corden,
"The Tariff," The Economics of Australian Industry,
ed. Alex Hunter (Melbourne: Melbourne University
Press, 1963); Balassa, op. cit. Some of Basevi's
preliminary data were cited in UNCTAD document
TD/B/AC.1/1 and Corr. 1, "Preferences: Review of
Discussions."

32. There are a variety of forms of the formula
which can be used to calculate effective rates.
Corden has used one:

$ER = \dfrac{t - \bar{t}i}{v}$, where ER is the effective rate of protection, t the nominal tariff, $\bar{t}$ the average tariff
on material inputs, i the value of material inputs
as a per cent of total value, and v the value added
as a per cent of total value. Some of the principal
relationships which emerge from this and other comparable formulae for calculating effective rates are:
where $t = \bar{t}$, then ER = t; where $t > \bar{t}$, then $ER > \bar{t}$;
and where $t < \bar{t}$, then $ER < t$. Since inputs usually
carry lower rates than final products in all tariff
structures, the normal case is the second where
$t > \bar{t}$, and therefore where the effective rate is
greater than the nominal rate.

33.   "Survey of Progress in the Reduction and
Elimination of Barriers Affecting Products Examined
by Committee III," Com. III/119, October 21, 1963.

34.   Alvin H. Hansen, The Dollar and the International Monetary System (New York: McGraw-Hill,
1965), pp. 17, 19.   Lawrence B. Krause, "United
States Imports and the Tariff," American Economic
Review, XLIX, No. 2 (May, 1959), 542-51, argued that
as of that date large tariff reductions were needed
to increase United States foreign trade.   There are,
of course, contrary points of view on the role of
price elasticity, e.g., Arnold C. Harberger, "Some
Evidence on the International Price Mechanism," The
Journal of Political Economy, LXV, No. 6 (December,
1957), 506-21.

35.   Gunnar Myrdal, Challenge to Affluence (New
York: Pantheon, 1962-63), p. 145.   Myrdal has discussed the trade and development issues of the underdeveloped countries in An International Economy,
Problems and Prospects (New York: Harper & Brothers,
1956); Rich Lands and Poor: The Road to World Prosperity (New York: Harper & Brothers, 1957); and in
a foreword in Hansen's book, op. cit., he advocates
discriminatory treatment in favor of the underdeveloped countries.

36.   Gottfried Haberler, A Survey of International Trade Theory, International Finance Section,
Princeton University, 1961, p. 57.

37.   TD/B/C.2/1/Add.1 and TD/B/AC.1/4/Add.1,
Annex B, p. 18.

38.   Patterson, op. cit., p. 30.

39.   This point is not idly made.   In discussions with United States Government officials, some
labor and industry people who said they did not mind
preferences coupled this with the statement that
they had in mind something like the cotton-textile
agreement, namely, preferences coupled with absolute
quotas.

40.   6 UST 2981, Article III, from Paragraphs 2
and 3 of the Agreement.   The emphasis is supplied.

41.   Towards a New Trade Policy for Development,
p. 62.

42. Hansen, op. cit., p. 142.

43. Patterson, op. cit., pp. 25-28.

44. TD/B/C.2/1/Add.1 and TD/B/AC.1/4/Add.1, Annex B, p. 47.

45. For example, with regard to the Philippine Trade Act of 1946 (H.R. 5856), in the hearings before the Committee on Finance, U.S. Senate, 79th Congress, 2d Session, April 2-6, 1946, Paul V. McNutt, U.S. High Commissioner to the Philippines, stated: "Actually, while this bill takes the form of a tariff bill and has to do with duties and imposts, it is, in fact, a realistic approach to the rehabilitation of the Philippines which happens to take this form." (p. 91)

46. TD/B/C.2/1/Add.1 and TD/B/AC.1/4/Add.1, Annex B, p. 23.

47. Towards a New Trade Policy for Development, p. 67.

48. 1961 data, Statistical Office of the United Nations, unpublished.

49. United Nations, The Growth of World Industry, 1938-1961, National Tables (New York, 1963), document ST/STAT/SER.P/2.

50. The United Kingdom learned this at the United Nations General Assembly in December, 1965. Despite the United Kingdom preference position at UNCTAD and since, this did not prevent some twenty-five African countries from leaving the Assembly hall during Prime Minister Wilson's speech on Rhodesia on December 16 in the very same week that the Assembly was approving a resolution on UNCTAD on December 20.

51. Towards a New Trade Policy for Development, p. 69.

52. TD/B/C.2/1/Add.1 and TD/B/AC.1/4/Add.1, Annex B, p. 45.

53. Memorandum Concerning Certain Items on the
Agenda of the United Nations Conference on Trade and
Development, submitted by France, document E/CONF.46/74,
February 27, 1964, p. 18.

54. Ibid., Corr. 1, p. 3.

55. UNCTAD, Preparatory Committee, Second Session, summary records of 34th meeting (E/CONF.46/PC/
SR.34). The speech in question was delivered in a
bitterly sarcastic tone. Rodrigues represented
Brazil at UNCTAD until the downfall of the Goulart
government in Brazil, which occurred during the Conference, after which Rodrigues also departed the
scene.

56. Public Law 87-794, October 11, 1962, Section 211.

57. Haberler, Theory of International Trade,
op. cit., p. 373.

5

WHAT THE PROPOSALS ARE

Selectivity of preferences can take a variety of forms. Preferences can be selective among preference-receiving countries, i.e., be granted to only one or some of the countries defined as less-developed, but not to all of them. Preferences can be selective by product. They can be selective on the part of the preference-giving countries, i.e., only one or some of the countries defined as developed, but not all or most of them, would grant preferences. The granting country might give different preferences to different countries, i.e., different as to product or as to margin of preference. Selectivity might refer to all of these aspects at the same time.

The crucial elements of selectivity relate to preference-giving and preference-receiving countries, namely, whether special relationships between particular developed and particular less-developed countries (or regions) are established which exclude other developed and less-developed countries (or regions). It is this country or regional aspect that the less-developed countries have principally in mind when they say that "preferences should be of general application,"[1] since even though they ask for tariff preferences on "all manufactures and semimanufactures,"[2] they recognize this as being unlikely.

The merging at the margins of general and selective preferences has been discussed elsewhere. As products accumulate in selectivity by product,

and as exceptions are made from a system of preferences generalized to all products; as bilateral
preferences between particular developed and less-
developed countries build up; and as the margin of
preference is differentiated by stage of development
in a general system--as these things take place,
general and selective preferences have much similarity. But despite this similarity, the intent of the
two systems is different, and this can best be seen
by contrasting what the selective preference proponents advocate with what the general preference proponents have advocated (as discussed in the previous
chapter).

In the present international context, selective
preferences were first advocated by Maurice Brasseur,
then Belgian Minister for External Trade and Technical Assistance, on May 17, 1963, at a ministerial
meeting of the GATT.[3] The Brasseur plan, as it has
since come to be known, set forth a series of guide-
lines for the granting of preferences by developed
to less-developed countries. For industries in
which less-developed countries already are competitive, Brasseur not only did not suggest preferences,
but he advocated negotiated arrangements "to re-
store normal price competition" since "one must
. . . recognize that as a matter of policy no government can permit established industries at home to
be laid open to sudden and irresistible pressures of
competition against which it is impossible to fight
with normal trading weapons."

For industries in less-developed countries not
yet competitive, he asked for a gradually declining
level of preferences, during which time the import
protection in the developing country for these industries also would decline in order to "expose them
to international competition." These ideas were
later amplified: The preferences would result from
bilateral negotiation between the party granting and
the party receiving the preference; the preferences
would be selective by product as well as by country;
"no reciprocity would be sought by the party granting

the preference."[4]   There is some implication in
Brasseur's statement that "reciprocity" might be
asked in the sense of avoidance of market disruption
in the advanced countries from developing-country
exports of products in which they are already competitive.

The French are in favor of selective preferences along the lines of the Brasseur plan.[5]   France
has suggested "a concept of preferential tariffs
which are selective--as regards the countries which
grant them or benefit from them--and are temporary
and degressive as regards the products they affect."[6]
In its submission to the special committee on preferences, the French again underlined these same
words--selective, degressive, and temporary.[7]   The
French have emphasized the need to negotiate any
preferences, that preferences should be both tariff
and nontariff in nature, that preferences should not
encourage competitiveness because of low wages, and
that "the negotiation of a preference system should
involve the granting of reciprocal concessions."   It
is only on this last quoted portion that the overt
French and Belgian positions seem to differ.

It may be worth noting a point which will be
touched on again later, and which may have some future significance if the Brasseur plan, or some
close variant of it, ever is to become a reality,
namely, that the EEC countries do not have one position.   Germany has indicated its willingness to support a general preference system; the Germans have
been less than precise as to what this means, except
that it does not mean a selective system.   The Dutch
have said they favor a general system, and the Ital-
ians, more equivocally, have said the same.   If the
EEC is to have a common external tariff and grant
tariff preferences to developing countries, at some
stage there will have to be one position.

The Latin Americans repeatedly have stated
their support for general preference systems.   In
this they have followed the lead of Prebisch, the
erstwhile Executive Secretary of ECLA.   The Latin

American support for general preferences is explicit
in the Charter of Alta Gracia[8] and in subsequent declarations in support of the "economic and social as-
pirations and goals" of Alta Gracia.[9] But this call
for general preferences, while it has continued, has
taken some interesting twists. Roberto Campos of
Brazil has advocated the defensive use of selective
preferences between the United States and Latin
America to compensate for the discrimination Latin
America faces in the EEC. In a letter of August 10,
1965, from the Inter-American Committee on the Alliance for Progress (CIAP) to the Presidents of the
American Republics, the following passage appears:

> The fact is, however, that since the
> UNCTAD meeting the movement outside
> the hemisphere has been toward more
> rather than less preferences in trade,
> particularly in relation to tropical
> products. This tendency is damaging
> the prospects for the Alliance for
> Progress. Therefore, although we are
> opposed to the creation of spheres of
> influence, we commend for urgent con-
> sideration, a policy of transitory,
> defensive measures to compensate for
> such preferences. It is inequitable
> for the products of some of the devel-
> oping countries to enjoy preferences
> outside the hemisphere plus nondis-
> criminatory access to the U. S. market.
> A policy to compensate for such dis-
> crimination against Latin America
> should be worked out pragmatically, on
> a commodity-by-commodity basis, with
> provisions which would facilitate re-
> turn to nondiscriminatory trade as dis-
> criminating practices are removed else-
> where.[10]

One point noted in an earlier chapter and which
should be kept in mind in assessing this suggestion
is that the United States generally has no duties or
other import restrictions on the kind of products

(coffee, cocoa, bananas) for which compensatory
preferences are being suggested. In order to institute preferences, some restrictions would have to be
imposed, and this would affect traders in the United
States as well as the exporting countries which
would face new discrimination. It is simpler to introduce preferences by forgiveness from existing restrictions than to do so by imposing new restrictions.

Prebisch, who has made amply clear his support
for general preferences, has not really opposed the
type of compensatory preferences suggested by Campos
or in the CIAP letter. For example, the following
passage appears in a speech he made in Viña del Mar,
Chile:

> There are voices which say, "Well, let
> us try the preferential policy for those
> products which are subject in other re-
> gions of the world to a preferential
> policy." Good, that is a tactical po-
> sition. If this tactical position helps
> the fundamental objective of bringing
> about the dissolution of those prefer-
> ential systems which exist today, as
> that of Africa and that of the British
> Commonwealth, if that tactic has this
> effect, I would have nothing to say.
> But if on the other hand, it means ini-
> tiating in Latin America a regional
> preferential policy, it would be very
> serious and I believe all those who
> have some responsibility to the govern-
> ments and popular opinion in Latin
> America, must speak with complete clar-
> ity and promptly to avoid the spread
> of this idea.[11]

Prebisch's position is not a tenable one, since
once a "tactic" of compensatory preferences of this
type were initiated, it is doubtful that the preferences would be eliminated if the tactic did not work
and the EEC and Commonwealth preferences continued.
Whether one calls it a tactic or a policy, new

selective preferences would come into existence.

The range of selective preference proposals thus covers those of the Belgian-French type, designed to be promoted as a deliberate policy; and those of the CIAP type, designed as a tactic to help eliminate selective preferences which already exist by first extending new selective preferences.

There is a school of thought which argues that while only general preferences are desirable, selective preferences must ultimately become general once the problems of discrimination among less-developed countries become intolerable. Just how long the time span must be before selective preferences become so intolerable as to be made into general ones is not clear and obviously is crucial. This is an argument hard to take seriously as a policy prescription; it is analogous to the argument that atomic destruction of the world must obviously ultimately lead to a better world than the world under destruction, so that over some unspecified long run, things must get better. The CIAP argument is not this naive; rather it says that Latin America wants either nondiscrimination or general preferences, but failing these, will accept selective preferences and then see what the outcome will be.

THE ECONOMIC CASE FOR AND AGAINST
SELECTIVE PREFERENCES

In all discussions of general preferences, two fundamental issues tend to cloud the picture: What should be done about products in which particular less-developed countries, or less-developed countries in general, already are competitive? How can preferences help the least-developed of the developing countries?

Australia has made the first point explicit in its principle of "competitive need." Brasseur did the same in his discussion of market disruption. France has done the same by pointing out that "some products do not require preferential treatment."[12]

The second point pervades all discussion of
preferences. The less-developed of the developing
countries have raised it. This was a basic point
even in the early GATT discussion of preferences by
developed to less-developed countries. For example,
in the report of the GATT working party on preferences of October, 1963, the following sentence appears:

> It was also suggested that account
> should be taken of the fact that the
> less-developed countries themselves
> were at differing stages of develop-
> ment, perhaps by granting preferences
> on a sliding scale linked to per capita
> income with larger preferences for
> countries with a per capita income of,
> say, less than $150 per annum.[13]

Prebisch noted "that the problem of the least developed countries as regards preferential arrangements
is a very real one and that the issue must be faced
squarely." He later added that "This is not . . .
a matter on which a dogmatic position can be taken;
it is par excellence, one of the most important
questions calling for further analysis and discussion."[14]

The strength of the selective preference approach is that it meets both problems. By giving
preferences selectively by product, only products
not now competitive, but where the prospects for future competitiveness exist, need be selected. By
giving preferences selectively by country, less- or
more-developed among the developing countries can be
chosen for the industry in question.

There is an additional powerful economic argument for selective preferences, namely, that a more
reasonable assurance can be given that it will work
for the industry in question. If only a given industry is chosen in a single developing country, and

this industry is assured preference for x yea
all other foreign competitors, this might st.
the necessary investment; a general preference ᴐ
might be considerably more amorphous. It might even
be that the proponents of selective preferences had
particular foreign investments in mind and wanted to
assure some preferential access to their home markets
before proceeding. If the aim is to develop particular industries in particular developing countries,
this is an important consideration.

The Brasseur plan has another important advantage in that it ties preferences to gradual reduction of import tariffs by the less-developed country
so that the industry in question might develop the
necessary competitiveness both at home and abroad.
A good deal has been written about the excessive protection afforded many industries in less-developed
countries with the result that the industries never
develop competitiveness abroad, and indeed, impede
the competitiveness of industry generally.[15] The
United States submission to the special committee on
preferences made this point:

> Developing countries . . . frequently
> find it necessary to protect infant in-
> dustries by extremely high tariffs,
> frequently 100 per cent ad valorem,
> or more, over long periods of time.
> There is no reason to believe that an
> industry that feels it needs substan-
> tial tariff protection from foreign
> competition in its home market will be
> able to overcome this same foreign com-
> petition in export markets with a pref-
> erence of, say, 10 per cent or less.[16]

Latin America exemplifies these high protective
import duties of 100 and 200 per cent ad valorem, or
higher. The precise tariff duties tend to overstate
the actual level of protection, since the high duties
also make allowance for overvalued exchange rates;
and these, in turn, impede exports. It probably is
significant, however, that of all the developing

areas, Latin America's manufactured exports loom
least large. They were 3 per cent of the total value of Latin American exports in 1955, 3 per cent in
1960, and 4 per cent in 1963; for developing countries as a whole, the rates were 8, 9, and 10 per
cent.[17] The ECLA secretariat has noted the lack
of competitiveness of Latin American industry due,
inter alia, to "the size of the market, often too
small for more than one or two enterprises, and
partly from tariff or quantitative protection which
is often tantamount to an embargo on imports."[18]

The point being made is that there is recognition in the Brasseur plan that overprotection in the
developing countries impedes their exports of manufactured goods; and that there is a way under a selective system to try to cure this defect on a case-
by-case basis.

It already has been noted that a great virtue
of trade as a device for making foreign exchange
available to developing countries is that trade is
self-policing. No matter what the developing country does after it gets aid, the aid already has
flowed in; under a trade device, the trade must take
place before the foreign exchange becomes available.
Selective preferences maximize this self-policing
mechanism since the trade can be pinpointed.

Selective preferences also have a type of
built-in protection against market disruption in the
developed country. For example, the procedure could
be to give preferences only up to a certain in-quota
level for the product in question, but then remove
all preferences when that level is exceeded on the
grounds that over-quota exports over most-favored-
nation tariffs demonstrate that even in-quota preferences are not necessary. This technique would
tend to put pressure on the developing country not
to exceed the preferential quota except in industries where increasing returns were abundantly self-
evident. This point was first suggested by a representative from a developed country.[19]

One possible economic defect of the selective
preference device is that it may attempt too much.
It would give an incentive for planners and investors in developed countries to decide in advance
which developing countries should get preferences
for which industries for export to which markets.
This type of advance decision between pairs of countries for particular industries would be repeated
over and over again. It is hard to believe, given
the probable politics of bilateral preference bargaining, that this is the most efficient way to decide on industry locations and on which developing
countries should get which industries.

But having said this, the point still remains
that a selective preference, for a favored industry
in a favored country, with some reasonable assurance
of access to at least one developed-country market,
does have a reasonable chance for economic success.
This, essentially, is the economic case in favor of
selective preferences.

THE POLITICAL CASE FOR AND AGAINST
SELECTIVE PREFERENCES

The political case for selective preferences
seems less good than the economic; and if the system
were to break down politically, it would also fail
in an economic sense.

The political disability which the United States
encountered in its earlier selective preference
(yclept conditional most-favored-nation) period was
recounted in Chapter 2 and will not be repeated. To
repeat one basic point, however: To treat some countries preferentially means to treat others discrimi-
natorily and unfavorably, and consequently to look
for political problems with the latter. This was
one reason the earlier selective preference system
broke down.

Viewed from the United States, however, there
are several political arguments militating in favor

of selective preferences. The first and most com-
pelling is that given in the CIAP letter cited earlier, namely, that other developed countries are
now giving selective preferences to certain less-
developed countries, thereby discriminating against
Latin American and other developing countries; and
in view of the important United States political
interest in Latin America, some compensatory action
on the part of the United States should be taken.
This compensatory action may perpetuate itself, in
which case different developing countries will have
preferential access to different developed-country
markets; or, this compensatory action may eventually lead to the elimination of all such selective
preferences.

The pressure for such compensation is great.
Many Latin Americans advocate it. There is some
sentiment for it in the United States Congress.[20]
Thomas Mann, formerly the Under Secretary of State
for Economic Affairs, had been reported as favoring
such a course.[21] Walt Rostow, then of the State Department, signed the CIAP letter in his CIAP status.
Walter Lippmann, as noted earlier, has attempted to
make a case for a special United States-Latin American relationship,[22] and it is not a far leap from
this special relationship to trade preferences. The
existence of the Alliance for Progress is in itself
a profound manifestation of the special relationship
which exists between the United States and Latin
America.

As a purely tactical matter, as a sort of game-
theory move, it seems clear that EEC-African and
United Kingdom-Commonwealth preferences will not
disappear merely as the result of United States ex-
hortations; the bargaining positions would be more
equal if some Latin American preferences into the
United States market existed.

It also has been argued by some that if trade
is a better mechanism than aid for helping less-
developed countries amass foreign exchange, then
perhaps trade should be used as a political weapon,

just as bilateral aid is sometimes so used. A bilateral selective preference provides such leverage.
It provides a way to turn on preferences when political relations are good; and to turn them off when
political relations are strained. France, for example, turned off its purchases of Tunisian wine in
just this manner. Having done this once, the cred-
ibility that it will be done again may of itself
have a restraining effect on political actions by a
developing country receiving preferences which are
adverse to the interests of the developed country
granting such preferences.

This is a blunt political weapon, and it has
its major weaknesses. Just as bilateral aid is subject to blackmail pressure from developing countries,
so too would bilateral preferences be. Indeed, the
blackmail potential may be greater in the trade
field since cutting off trade affects not only the
developing country but also the importers in the developed country, the users of the imported product,
and in many cases the foreign investors in the developing country. Trade is not as flexible a device
as aid; once a preference is given, it is harder to
turn off than aid, since vested interests in the
preference-giving country also are involved.

Thus, the political pressure in a system of
bilateral preferences would operate in both direc-
tions--the developed country would have a potential
threat to prevent behavior it disliked and the developing country would have a lever for blackmail,
first to get preferences, and second to maintain
them in the face of all but the most flagrant disre-
gard of the sensibilities of the developed country.

The Walter Lippmann thesis that the United
States should concentrate its financial effort in
Latin America rather than in the entire less-
developed or third world also has been used to argue that trade preferences should be given to Latin
America. However, the logic in this instance seems
to break down. One might reduce United States aid
to Asia and Africa and concentrate more on Latin

America; but if one were to do this, which presumably is what Lippmann is advocating, one really cannot at the same time reduce Asian and African trading opportunities in the United States. The reverse might be argued, that if aid to Asia and Africa were to be reduced, these countries should be given even greater opportunities to earn their way by trade.

The major political disability of bilateral selective preferences, or regional ones, is the sphere-of-influence argument, and the analogy to neocolonialism. It is far from clear that the EEC-African relationship is a stable one politically, and that the United States need take any special steps to counter it. It is even less clear that a special United States-Latin American trade relationship would be stable.

George Lodge has cited the following statement of Eduardo Frei, the President of Chile, whom he has described as "probably the outstanding statesman in Latin America today":

> The central tenet of Christian Democracy is the belief that we are witnesses to the crisis of a world exhausted, to the death of paternalism, and to the birth of a civilization of work and solidarity with man as its center, rather than the pursuit of monetary gain that pervaded the bourgeois society. And its inspiration is that this new era in history and the new social condition will be based on Christian values and concepts of Christianity.[23]

Spheres-of-influence and special relationships between a developed and less-developed country do smack of paternalism, and probably would not be durable, or conducive of good relations even while they lasted. As noted earlier, the United States-Cuban experience is a good illustration of this.

Human relations, like intercountry relations, operate most harmoniously when necessities are obtained as a matter of right rather than of privilege. Organized charity gave way to governmental social security systems; private schools gave way to public schools; sufferance of Negroes in white schools is giving way to integration as a basic civil right. The sufferance of less-developed countries' exports is a less healthy system than their right to trade as equals; a junior trading partner being patronized by the developed country acting as a senior partner is not likely to last. A system of one-way selective preferences is a form of noblesse oblige, and probably inherently unstable. A general system of preferences is somewhat less patronizing, but still not completely divorced from this paternalistic atmosphere.

The paternalistic attitude might be lessened if the preferences were reciprocal rather than one-way. Perhaps this is what the French have in mind by their insistence on reciprocity.[24] Thus, there is some advocacy of a United States-Latin American free-trade area as much in conformity with Article XXIV of the GATT as are the EEC free-trade areas with associated African countries. This will be treated in the next section.

The paternalism also could be lessened if some day it becomes possible to organize the world the way individual countries now are organized, in which, e.g., richer areas pay taxes for services to poorer areas, or in which governments deliberately seek to procure goods and services from depressed areas. Preferential treatment to poor areas within countries is possible under nationalistic circumstances which do not now exist internationally.

In concluding this section on the political advantages and disabilities of selective preferences for the United States, it is clear that the arguments are not all one-sided. There are some distinct political advantages, particularly in view of the fact that the developing area with which the

United States has the closest relations, Latin America, now faces active discrimination. But there are
also severe political disadvantages, and for a country like the United States with worldwide interests,
these are indeed formidable.

A UNITED STATES-LATIN AMERICA
FREE-TRADE AREA

The history of the earlier attempts at a free-
trade area between the United States and Latin America was outlined in Chapter 2. These earlier attempts were of no interest to Latin America since
its exports to the United States, mainly primary
products, already could enter the United States either free of duty or at low rates, while United
States manufactured exports to Latin America would
benefit from lower duties.

This situation has not changed. In 1963, about
90 per cent of United States imports from Latin America were in SITC categories 0 through 4 (essentially
primary products), while about 75 per cent of United
States exports to Latin America were in SITC categories 5 through 8 (essentially manufactures).[25] Of
Latin America's manufactured exports to the United
States in 1963, about 30 per cent by value was made
up of unwrought copper from Chile; copper, special
textile fabrics, and unwrought lead made up 50 per
cent of Latin America's total manufactured exports
to the United States.

This, of course, is a static picture and merely
says that free entry to the United States would not
particularly benefit Latin America if its present
economic structure were maintained; it says nothing
about the kinds of industries that might be established if preferential free entry were to be achieved.

The kind of free-trade area that might be of
interest to Latin America is one that gives Latin
America free entry to the United States, particularly for manufactured goods, with some specified exceptions and safeguards for the United States. In

return, Latin America would give free entry to United States products, particularly manufactured goods, whenever these goods had to be imported. The reason for the emphasis is that this device would permit Latin America to develop its own industries, since in these industries the goods produced would not have to be imported. This is the nature of the exception from free trade which the associated African countries enjoy in their relations with the EEC. If the EEC-associated African countries' arrangement under the Yaounde Convention is consistent with the GATT Article XXIV, so would a similar United States-Latin American relationship be consistent.

The advantages of such an arrangement are that it would give Latin America trade advantages similar to those enjoyed by several other developing areas; it would not prevent internal Latin American industrial development, but would give the United States preferential entry only over other exporters, particularly those in Europe and Japan; it would permit the foreign-investment potential of selective preferences to operate in Latin America; it would be reciprocal and thus eliminate the most flagrant patronizing aspect of selective preferences, while at the same time it would have more appeal to the United States Congress since it would involve a quid pro quo; and it could be devised to promote Latin American regional economic integration.

With respect to this last point, such an arrangement would be consistent with suggestions made by William L. Clayton and Senator Javits for a hemispheric free-trade area or customs union.[26] It is compatible, also, with remarks made recently by José Garrido Torres of Brazil to the plenary meeting of ECLA, in which the hope was expressed that "in the not too distant future, the integrated zone might include the entire hemisphere."[27]

But there are major shortcomings to this kind of free-trade area between the United States and Latin America. In the earlier attempts at a free-trade area in the nineteenth century, the Latin

Americans emphasized the need not to disrupt their trading relations with Europe. This is still true. Table 8 gives the value of Latin American trade in recent years.

TABLE 8

The Direction of Latin America's Trade, 1959-63

(Millions of dollars, approximate)

Latin American Imports (f.o.b.)

Year	From All Sources	From the U.S. and Canada	From Western Europe		
			Total	EEC	EFTA
1959	7,580	3,680	2,440	1,510	830
1960	7,820	3,630	2,590	1,560	900
1961	8,080	3,570	2,730	1,720	900
1962	8,090	3,370	2,630	1,630	860
1963	7,960	3,350	2,430	1,500	800

Latin American Exports

Year	To All Destinations	To the U.S. and Canada	To Western Europe		
			Total	EEC	EFTA
1959	8,290	3,820	2,510	1,430	950
1960	8,610	3,740	2,730	1,580	1,010
1961	8,710	3,420	2,770	1,610	980
1962	9,170	3,590	3,010	1,830	990
1963	9,750	3,710	3,330	2,030	1,050

Source: U.N. Monthly Bulletin of Statistics, March, 1965.

What the figures show are that with preferences, the United States probably could replace some European exports to Latin America; but more crucially, this replacement might be at the expense of Latin

America's exports to Europe, which are increasing
far more substantially than are Latin America's exports to the United States and Canada.

Another major shortcoming of a United States-
Latin American free-trade area, apart from sphere-
of-influence considerations, is that it ignores
United States relations with other developing countries and areas. It would not make sense to help
Latin American trade if this, in turn, would adversely affect Indian, or Pakistani, or Filipino,
or Thai, or Taiwanese, etc., manufactured exports
to the United States. Additionally, the "orphan"
argument must be considered; if there are special
trade relationships between Europe and Africa, and
the United Kingdom and the Commonwealth, and the
United States and Latin America, who watches out
for the orphan countries (the Philippines, Thailand,
Indonesia, and others) who are discriminated against
and who have no special market?

At the present time, the case for a special
United States-Latin American trade relationship,
which might take the form of a free-trade area, does
not seem persuasive. But it should not be foreclosed.

It was noted earlier in the discussion of general preferences that further proliferation of selective preferences, particularly between the EEC
and less-developed countries, might alter the present equation. One assumes that the French and Belgian advocacy of selective preferences is not designed to cement the relationship between the EEC
and the associated African states, since preferences
already exist in these cases under the alleged sanction of the GATT Article XXIV. Therefore, the logical
assumption is that any new selective preferences
which the EEC might enter into would be with other
countries. These might include Latin America.
This, of course, would be both an economic and political step; and it certainly would alter the
equation.

In order for the EEC to enter into new preferential tariff arrangements, a common EEC policy would be needed. At present different EEC countries have different attitudes toward preferences. Given this need for a common position, and given also the importance of the United States-European relationship, it is hard to believe that the EEC as a whole would enter into special preferences with particular Latin American countries if the United States made abundantly clear that it would react strongly and adversely to such arrangements. The reaction, of course, could take many forms, both in Europe and elsewhere.

What does seem clear is that it behooves the United States to remain flexible on this issue of an arrangement with Latin America, both in its own protection and in the protection of Latin American interests.

THE ADMINISTRATIVE CASE FOR AND AGAINST SELECTIVE PREFERENCES

If there were many bilateral selective preferences, this could become an administrative nightmare. The arithmetic cited earlier with regard to tariff quotas is even more applicable for selective preferences, namely, that if 20 developed countries made arrangements with 80 less-developed countries for only 100 tariff items (which seems like a small number of items), this would give 160,000 preferences. With selective preferences, pressure on the part of buyers to open new preferential sources would be great; and pressure by sellers for preferred markets would be equally great. Everybody would be on the alert to keep abreast of the bilateral preferential negotiations in process so as not to be foreclosed out of markets or potential sources of supply. The system could become extremely complex.

But having said this, one must also admit that most-favored-nation tariff structures have become extremely complex, in part for the express purpose

of giving selective preferences while ostensibly using the most-favored-nation system. Haberler, among
others, has noted that one "reason for the increasing complication of tariff schedules is the effort
to evade the most-favored-nation clause."[28] Kindleberger has referred to this same point, that "Part
of the effect of the most-favored-nation clause was
lost by reclassification: the limiting of concessions to new and narrow classes so defined as to exclude the products of competing countries."[29] Viner
has argued that there is much exaggeration of the
extent to which such evasion of most-favored-nation
obligations is practiced by splitting tariff classifications since this would give rise "to the danger
of the termination of amicable tariff relations with
the countries suffering from such evasion."[30]

The conclusions regarding the administration of
a selective preference system are: that it would be
messy if there were many bilateral preferences; that
an explicit selective preference system probably
would be messier than the selective preferences in-
herent in splitting of tariff classifications under
a most-favored-nation system since there are limits
to the latter; but that a selective system would be
manageable if the number of bilateral agreements
were kept limited. In short, the argument for or
against selective preferences really cannot stand or
fall on administrative arguments alone.

CONCLUDING COMMENTS ON SELECTIVE PREFERENCES

The economic ability to pinpoint the benefits in
the countries and industries selected by the preference givers and receivers is alluring, and this is
the principal virtue of a system of selective preferences. In the case of the United States and Latin
America, whether the selective preferences were of a
regional nature based on a form of free-trade area
or of a purely defensive nature to give Latin America compensatory preferences for the same products
for which it faces discrimination in the EEC, there

is considerable political appeal to selective preferences. If one is looking toward a possible future
hemispheric free-trade area or customs union, selective preferences to Latin America, whether bilateral or one-way, might be a good starting point.

Viewed from the vantage of United States policy, the foregoing are important considerations.
But they must be weighed against the potential disadvantages. The United States has learned that
there is a tremendous political cost to selective
preferences (and hence to selective discrimination
against other countries), and it would be folly to
ignore this past history completely. In addition,
a special trading relationship between an advanced
and an underdeveloped country is perforce paternalistic and probably unstable.

Weighing the advantages against the disadvantages, the conclusion is that the United States
should not now enter into selective preferences and
should oppose the proliferation of selective preferences between other developed countries or areas and
less-developed countries.

It is this final point, however, which may turn
out to be the key one. Should the United States
fail in this effort to prevent proliferation, it may
be desirable to join the preference group, either
through a system of selective preferences, or perhaps
by a system of general preferences of the variety
suggested in the previous chapter. The major policy
recommendation, therefore, is that while not changing
its policy now, it behooves the United States to be
flexible and to be able to shift policy rapidly if so
required.

Notes to Chapter 5

1. The quoted words are from the developing countries' submission to the special committee on preferences, TD/B/C.2/1/Add.1 and TD/B/AC.1/4/Add.1, June 8, 1965, Annex B., p. 44.

2. _Ibid_.

3. GATT/750, May 17, 1963, press release.

4. TD/B/C.2/1/Add.1 and TD/B/AC.1/4/Add.1, Annex B, pp. 68-69.

5. Indeed, some people have suggested that the French as much as the Belgians were the originators of the Brasseur plan.

6. UNCTAD document E/CONF.46/74, February 27, 1964, Memorandum Concerning Certain Items on the Agenda of the United Nations Conference on Trade and Development, submitted by France, p. 20. Emphasis in original.

7. TD/B/C.2/1/Add.1 and TD/B/AC.1/4/Add.1, Annex B, p. 41.

8. UNCTAD document E/CONF.46/100, April 10, 1964.

9. The quoted words are from the Final Act of the Second Special Inter-American Conference signed in Rio de Janeiro, November 30, 1965. To put the Alta Gracia charter into context, it is coupled in the foregoing passage with such inter-American documents as the Act of Bogota and the Charter of Punta del Este; the Alta Gracia charter was a Latin American and not an inter-American document.

10. Letter reproduced in Latin American Development and Western Hemisphere Trade, Hearings before the Subcommittee on Inter-American Relationships of the Joint Economic Committee of the United States Congress, September 8-10, 1965, pp. 220-28.

11.   Speech of March 22, 1965, unofficial trans-
lation as reported in Department of State airgram
A-894 of April 9, 1965, from the American Embassy in
Santiago, Chile.

12.   TD/B/C.2/1/Add.1 and TD/B/AC.1/4/Add.1,
Annex B, p. 41.

13.   GATT, L/2073, October 24, 1963, Paragraph
14.

14.   Towards a New Trade Policy for Development,
Report by the Secretary-General of the United Nations
Conference on Trade and Development, United Nations,
New York, 1964, pp. 73-74.

15.   An excellent article on this subject with
respect to Latin America is Santiago Macario, "Protectionism and Industrialization in Latin America,"
Economic Bulletin for Latin America, IX, No. 1
(March, 1964), 61-102.

16.   TC/B/C.2/1/Add.1 and TD/B/AC.1/4/Add.1,
Annex B, p. 16.

17.   ECOSOC document E/4059, June 29, 1965.

18.   UNCTAD document E/CONF.46/71, February 27,
1964, on Latin America and the United Nations Conference on Trade and Development, prepared for UNCTAD
by the ECLA secretariat. The document in question
was originally prepared for an ECLA experts meeting
in Brasilia from January 20-25, 1964, which in turn
prepared the groundwork for the meeting at Alta
Gracia in Argentina under the auspices of the Inter-
American Economic and Social Council, which issued
the often-cited Charter of Alta Gracia.

19.   Privately to the author.

20.   See Latin American Development and Western
Hemisphere Trade, op. cit.

21.   For example, see Business Week, the International Outlook" column of January 23, 1964. Mann's reported advocacy of United States preferences for Latin America was on the grounds of strengthening the Alliance for Progress.

22.   See Chap. 2.

23.   George C. Lodge, "Revolution in Latin America," Foreign Affairs, XLIV, No. 2 (January, 1966), 173-97. The quotation is on p. 181. The emphasis is supplied.

24.   The suspicion is that the French are insisting on some reciprocity in order to maintain the preference they now enjoy in francophone Africa, since if they gave one-way preferences to other less-developed countries, they could hardly refuse to do the same for former territories.

25.   Data from OECD, Statistical Bulletin, Series C.

26.   See Latin American Development and Western Hemisphere Trade, op. cit., pp. 170 and 211-19.

27.   Information document 41, from speech of May 11, 1965, at Mexico City. The relevant sentences from the speech in Spanish are the following: "El Gobierno del Brasil considera que el mercado común cuya creación consideramos debe incluir sólo a la América Latina, vistas las grandes diferencias entre los niveles de ingreso de las naciones latino-americanas, por un lado, y de los Estados Unidos y el Canadá, por otro. Sin embargo, el proceso de integración debe ser lo suficientemente ambicioso como para permitir que, en un plazo relativamente corto, los países de la región alcancen grados de eficiencia y productividad equiparables a los de estos dos últimos países, para que en un futuro no muy lejano la zona integrada incluya todo el hemisferio."

28. Gottfried von Haberler, The Theory of International Trade (New York: Macmillan, 1936), p. 339.

29. Charles P. Kindleberger, International Economics (Homewood, Illinois: Richard D. Irwin, Inc., 1963), p. 239. In a footnote to this sentence, Kindleberger cites the classic example of a German concession to Switzerland on cows in a 1902 agreement: "large dapple mountain cattle or brown cattle reared at a spot at least 300 meters above sea level and having at least one month's grazing each year at a spot at least 800 meters above sea level."

30. Jacob Viner, "The Most-Favored-Nation Clause in American Commercial Treaties," The Journal of Political Economy, XXXII, No. 1 (February, 1924), 101-29. Quoted passage pp. 109-10.

6

PREFERENCES IN TRADE AMONG UNDERDEVELOPED COUNTRIES

PRESENT LEGAL STATUS AND ACTION PROPOSALS

This is the third of the three aspects of the trade-preference issue. To recapitulate, the three are: developed-country preferences generalized for exports, particularly of manufactures, from all underdeveloped countries; developed-country preferences given to selected exports from selected underdeveloped countries; preferences in trade among underdeveloped countries. The third aspect has been the least discussed in the recent international debate, yet, in a sense, it is the most important and the aspect which holds the greatest promise for the future. Economic integration among developing countries, in the form of sector arrangements, free-trade areas, customs unions, payments unions, and even economic unions, are forms of preferences by developing countries in trade inter se.

One can't avoid the feeling that this is the least discussed aspect of preferences because it requires action principally by developing countries themselves; the other forms of preferences depend primarily on action by the rich countries, and it's easier to discuss what somebody else should do. However, the issues in this field are complex; economic integration among less-developed countries is harder to achieve than among developed ones.

The basic international rules for preferences in trade among less-developed countries are the same as those for trade among developed countries, or between the two groups--namely, those embodied in the General Agreement on Tariffs and Trade. While all non-Communist developed countries with the exception of

Switzerland are full contracting parties to the GATT
(Switzerland has acceded provisionally), the same is
not true of less-developed countries; and a country
not affiliated with the GATT obviously is not bound
by it. Depending on one's definition, however, about
43 to 45 of the 66 full contracting parties (as of
early 1966) are less-developed, and about 10 of the
other 13 countries which participate in the work of
the Contracting Parties, or have acceded provisionally, or which maintain a de facto application, are
less-developed.[1] Therefore, the GATT provisions do
apply to most developing countries, particularly the
most important trading ones among them.

The basic GATT provision on preferences is Article I, the no-new-preference rule. Article XXIV, as
noted in Chapter 1, provides an exception to this
for a customs union or free-trade area, or interim
agreements leading to these, in which "duties and
other restrictive regulations of commerce . . . are
eliminated with respect to substantially all the
trade between the constituent territories of the
union or at least with respect to substantially all
the trade in products originating in such territories."[2] As already noted, there is no definition of
what constitutes "substantially all the trade."

This point has been of some significance. For
years it has been alleged that this all-or-nothing
rule (really a substantially-all-or-nothing rule)--
i.e., preferences on substantially all trade or no
preferences at all--could not be met in free-trade
areas or customs unions among less-developed countries. The Latin American Free-Trade Association
found difficulty meeting this rule, and in fact never
did fully--but for that matter, it is hard to believe
that the European Free-Trade Association, with its
exclusion of agriculture and special exemptions for
Portugal, or the Yaounde Convention between the EEC
and eighteen associated African countries, or the
EEC-Greece, or EEC-Turkey association agreements, do
meet this rule either. The GATT, however, has been flexible. Prebisch has noted: "Such was the experience
of the Latin American Free Trade Association which
might possibly not have been established had it not

been for this flexibility. This flexibility also existed in the case of other groupings."[3]

An even more revealing assertion of the GATT's flexibility in dealing with customs unions and free-trade
areas is the statement to its legislature by the New
Zealand Government with respect to the New Zealand-
Australia Free-Trade Agreement of August 31, 1965.
After explaining the nature of Article XXIV and re-
counting the GATT handling of some recent free-trade
area and customs union proposals put before it for
approval, such as the EEC, EFTA, LAFTA, and the EEC-
African association agreements, only one substantive
comment is made with regard to obtaining the GATT sanction: "In no case have the Contracting Parties rejected such a proposal."[4] In point of fact, the Contracting Parties have never either accepted or rejected any proposed agreement put before them under
Article XXIV. For all practical purposes, therefore,
if countries entering into free-trade or customs-
union agreements believe they meet the "substantially
all" rule, and so assert, the Contracting Parties are
likely to live and let live.

A good deal has been written both defending and
attacking the GATT rule. Clair Wilcox defended it
on the grounds that a customs union expands world
trade while a preferential area does not.[5] Isaiah
Frank has accepted this argument, mainly on the
grounds that an across-the-board reduction in trade
barriers required under the substantially-all-or-
nothing rule does not permit countries to pick and
choose among products and thus be able to give concessions where they won't hurt.[6] Dell criticizes
the all-or-nothing standard, which he argues was
drawn up with the rich countries in mind and has little relevance to the poor countries.[7] Viner has commented on the illogical position of "some supposed
virtue in a 100 per cent preference, which suddenly
turns to maximum evil at 99 per cent."[8] In view of the
GATT's flexibility to date, these defenses of and
attacks on the Article XXIV rule have an air of un-
reality.

To eliminate this issue as far as less-developed

countries were concerned, the United States "suggested in the GATT in November 1963 that consideration
be given to amending the GATT so as to permit developing countries to undertake regional economic integration on a broad sectoral basis."[9] This was a
recognition that sector preferences might be more
practicable than across-the-board preferences for
less-developed countries. The United States pushed
this point even further in the context of the Alliance for Progress. In remarks commemorating the
fourth anniversary of the Alliance, President Johnson said on August 17, 1965:

> In addition, I hope the American nations
> will consider the establishment of a pro-
> gram--patterned after the European Coal
> and Steel Community--for the production
> and trade, on a continental basis, of
> fertilizer, pesticides, and other prod-
> ucts that are needed to increase agri-
> cultural production. My country stands
> willing to help in such a venture.[10]

What was proposed, therefore, was that along-
side the Article XXIV substantially-all-or-nothing
rule, another rule be placed for less-developed coun-
tries--that they be encouraged to pick and choose
sector preferences. The European Coal and Steel
Community, cited as a desirable example by President
Johnson, itself contravened Article I without con-
forming to Article XXIV and was sanctioned only by a
GATT waiver.[11] The agreement of January 16, 1964,
between the United States and Canada for free trade
between the two countries in automobiles and original
parts therefor also required a waiver of its GATT
obligations by the United States. Under the 1963
United States proposal, sectoral agreements of this
type between less-developed countries would be consistent with the GATT without a waiver.

Article 15 of the abortive Havana Charter for
an international trade organization would have permitted preferential agreements for economic development under certain safeguards. Article 15 was the
basic model for the proposal made to the GATT by the

United States in 1963 and cited by Solomon. This
United States proposal has not yet been acted on,
which is a good indication that the developing countries really don't find the substantially-all-or-
nothing rule too onerous in practice. In 1954, Chile
had proposed the incorporation of Article 15 of the
Havana Charter into the GATT, which was not accepted.[12]

One provision of Article 15 is that the territories of the parties to such preferential agreements
be "contiguous one with another, or all parties be-
long to the same economic region."[13] An interpretive
note to this states that: "The Organization need not
interpret the term 'economic region' to require close
geographical proximity if it is satisfied that a sufficient degree of economic integration exists between
the countries concerned."

This is a point of some controversy. Even though
the basic instrument, the GATT, has not formally been
modified to permit sector preferences for less-
developed countries, this general position is now accepted; the kind of safeguards to accompany these
sector preferences remains unsettled. A country
like India, which may not be able to reach preferential agreements with its neighbor Pakistan for political and other reasons, has doubts about the Article
15 safeguard that preferences be exchanged only among
countries "contiguous one with another" or in "the
same economic region." The United States has felt
that the regional cooperation aspect of preferences
was perhaps the most crucial; President Johnson spoke
of sector preferences in Latin America, on the model
of the European Coal and Steel Community, not preferences between, say, Paraguay and Mali.

This point of controversy arose at the first
UNCTAD as well as in the GATT. Thus, with respect to
the UNCTAD recommendation on this subject, the United
States appended the following observation:

> The United States joined in the adoption
> by consensus of the Recommendation in
> Annex A.III.8 concerning promotion of
> trade in manufactures and semi-manufactures

among developing countries as it favors
efforts of developing countries in the
same economic region to join together
to form larger markets and to co-operate
to achieve accelerated economic development.   It does not, however, support the
principle that developing countries
which are not engaged in this close regional co-operation for development to
enter into discriminatory trade relationships of the kind apparently envisaged
by the terms of certain provisions of
the Recommendation.[14]

What lies behind this issue is whether less-
developed countries should be restricted in any way
in exchanging preferences, or whether preferential
trade has a deeper purpose, namely, to promote some
degree of economic integration. Were India and
Brazil, just to name two countries, permitted to
bilaterally negotiate preferences between them, particularly if the resultant preferences then were extended generally to all other less-developed countries as some have proposed, this obviously would
have an important limiting effect on Brazil's ability to enter into a preferential regional arrangement in Latin America. Chile could not have an exclusive LAFTA preference in Brazil if India or
Pakistan or the United Arab Republic, or all of them
plus all other less-developed countries, enjoyed
that same preference. This is the core of the issue
of regional versus wide-open preferences among developing countries; the two are ultimately incompatible.

The foregoing, then, are the proposals extant
for preferences among developing countries: to
legally permit sector preferences; whether preferences should be on a regional basis to promote integration, or whether preferences and increased intra-
developing-country trade are their own reward regardless of the economic integration potential involved.
Overlaying these issues are suggestions for preferences through regional payments unions along the
pattern of the European Payments Union, or through
regional quotas, along the patterns devised through
the Organization for European Economic Cooperation.[15]

UNITED STATES POLICY TOWARD
CUSTOMS UNIONS

Viner has noted: "Free-traders sometimes in almost the same breath disapprove of preferential reductions of tariffs but approve of customs unions,
which involve 100 per cent preference, and this is
the position at present of the United States Government and the doctrine of the Havana Charter."[16] As
noted, this is only partially true today; the United
States still thinks 100 per cent preferences (customs unions) are best, but is willing to see approaches among less-developed countries to this "best"
world through a "good" world of sector preferences.
Viner also has noted: "The literature on customs
unions in general, whether written by economists or
non-economists, by free-traders or protectionists,
is almost universally favorable to them, and only
here and there is a sceptical note to be encountered,
usually by an economist with free-trade tendencies."[17]
This is a prescient comment. For example, in the discussion of the recent United States-Canada automotive
products agreement, the editorial comment of the United States press was almost uniformly favorable, with
the exception of the Washington Post, which opposed
the agreement on the seeming grounds that it really
was not free trade.[18]

The United States position, stated simply, seems
to favor customs unions among developed countries, to
tolerate free-trade areas among developed countries,
and to favor both free-trade areas and customs unions
among underdeveloped countries. The almost uncriti-
cal support of customs unions seems to be based on
both economic and political grounds; the lukewarm
attitude toward free-trade areas among developed
countries, such as EFTA, seems to be based on the
grounds that the trade discrimination is not accompanied by potential political content; the support
of economic integration in any form among less-
developed countries is based on the hope that this
might have some political content, but is important
economically in any event.

All these premises are worth looking at, if only very briefly.

There was never any question but that the United States supported the EEC. The basic reason was political: As was believed regarding the OEEC, more so for NATO, even more so for the Coal-Steel Community, and most of all for the EEC, the United States wished to tie together Germany and France in the context of a Greater Europe so that the future would not repeat the past and so that the French and Germans would not initiate new wars against each other. It was argued by many that the EEC, being a customs union and even more so an economic union, must inevitably lead to greater political unity. This point was buttressed by the terms of the Rome treaty, under which as the EEC moved into successive stages more and more decisions could be reached by weighted as opposed to unanimous voting. The argument was that EFTA, being a mere trade arrangement, lacked this political content; and it generally has been believed that the United States would have been content to see EFTA die if the United Kingdom had succeeded in entering the Common Market.[19] On these same political grounds, the United States seemed to remain quite cold to possible Swiss and Swedish entrance into the EEC since, as neutrals, they could not but weaken the supranational aspects of EEC decision-making.

This is not the place to discuss the correctness of this political assumption. Viner, citing Schmöller and List, has noted that the historical evidence is against a commercial union leading to political union; with the possible exception of the German Zollverein, he has commented that political union either preceded or was simultaneous with commercial union.[20] Viner was writing before the formation of the EEC, which was designed as considerably more than a commercial union, so that the historical evidence may not necessarily be fully relevant. Nichols has written in a document appearing in December, 1965, at the very time that France was seeking some explicit elimination of weighted voting in the EEC when important national interests were

involved, that "the prospects for political unification are as good today, probably better, than they
have ever been."[21] According to press accounts, what
happened in January, 1966, among the Six was a tacit
EEC understanding that no country would be overruled
by weighted voting when it felt its vital interests
were involved, but that the Rome treaty provisions
would be left undisturbed. Since few really anticipated at this stage of European history that the
other five would really attempt to overrule either
France or Germany on a matter of vital national interest, despite the explicit provisions of the Rome
treaty, what seems to have happened was to accept
what was self-evident in any event, but to leave the
future to take care of itself by allowing the treaty
to remain undisturbed.

The conclusion one must reach, therefore, about
the EEC leading in time to political union, is that
this really is still an unknown. At the moment, the
prospects for political union look dim; in the future, as common budgetary receipts have to be used,
and even more if factor movements (capital, but particularly people) become really free, much greater
use of common decision-making will be inevitable.
The political premise on which the United States supported the EEC, therefore, may have been valid in
the mid-1950's, but this is uncertain; and it remains
uncertain in the mid-1960's.

The economic grounds for the United States support of the EEC (which seem to have largely been a
rationalization to back up the political decision already taken) was that with economic integration, economic growth would be greater than otherwise would
be the case; and that with greater growth, imports
from nonmembers would be greater with the discrimination than they would be with lesser growth and no
discrimination.

These are matters already thoroughly discussed
in the literature, and about which conclusions are
as murky as under the political premise of United
States policy. Balassa has contended that the business climate improved in the EEC with the widening

of the market, and that economic growth consequently
was greater than had been projected.[22]   In a more
analytical and empirical examination, Lamfalussy concluded: "There seem to be no obvious figures which
would point to a causal relationship between the establishment of the Common Market and the rapid growth
of its members."[23]   The United States business community, based on the belief that bigger and common markets are better markets, seems instinctively to take
the view expressed by Balassa that integration increases growth.[24]   In seeking membership in the EEC,
Prime Minister Macmillan argued that competition
would stimulate the United Kingdom's growth.

The figures by themselves prove nothing, since
they do not indicate what would have occurred had
the EEC not been established in 1958. As a matter
of information, the annual growth rates in gross
national product of the Six from 1954 to 1964 are
given in Table 9.

One thing that clearly has happened is that
intra-EEC trade has increased more rapidly than total
trade, although the latter also has increased substantially.

Like the political premise, the economic premise on which United States support for the EEC was
and is based is not really provable.

In a sense, neither the political nor economic
bases for the United States support of the EEC matter at this stage, since the EEC exists and, despite
its present tribulations, is a going concern.[25]
This look at the premises underlying United States
policy toward the EEC is instructive for examining
United States policy on integration among underdeveloped countries. This will be done by focusing
more on Latin America, where economic integration
has made most progress, than on other underdeveloped
regions.

TABLE 9

Annual Growth Rate of GNP, 1954-64
(Per cent change over previous year)

Year	Belgium	Luxembourg	France	Germany (FRG)[c]	Italy	Netherlands	Total EEC Countries
1955	5.2	3.6	5.2	11.5	6.7	7.4	7.9
1956	2.6	0.9	5.8	7.1	4.2	3.4	5.6
1957	2.7	4.9	5.1	5.9	6.3	3.2	5.3
1958	-0.9	1.5	3.1	3.5	4.4	-0.1	3.0
1959	2.7	1.5	2.7	7.0	7.3	5.2	5.3
1960	4.6	8.2	7.6	8.7	6.8	8.9	7.8
1961	4.5	2.6	4.5	5.4	8.4	3.5	5.5
1962	4.3	-2.3	6.6	4.1	6.3	2.6	5.2
1963	3.9	3.0	4.4	3.2	4.8	3.6	3.9
1964[a]	5.0	6.3	4.9	6.5	3.0	6.1	5.3
Total	40.3	34.2	62.4	83.8	75.7	53.3	70.2
Annual Average[b]	3.4	3.0	5.0	6.3	5.8	4.4	5.5

Source: Compiled by A. I. D. Percentages based on 1962 constant prices.

[a]Preliminary. [b]Geometric average. [c]Includes West Berlin.

TABLE 10

Intra-EEC Trade as Per Cent of Total Trade

Country	1958		1964	
	Exports	Imports	Exports	Imports
Belg.-Lux.	45	47	63	53
France	22	22	39	37
Italy	24	21	38	33
Netherlands	42	42	56	52
Germany (FRG)	27	26	36	35

Source: EEC statistics. Figures derived from volumes for appropriate years of Foreign Trade,
Analytical Tables, Statistical Office of
the European Communities.

The immediate motives of the Latin American economic integration movements--both of the Latin American Free-Trade Association (LAFTA) and the Central
American Common Market (CACM)--are to create larger
markets and to exploit thereby the opportunities of
modern scientific and technological research; to
strengthen the Latin American "capacity for effective negotiation"; and to secure "greater political
influence internationally."[26]   The Charter of Punta
del Este refers to "broadening of present national
markets," and "obtaining greater productivity through
specialized and complementary industrial production."[27]

The documents on Latin American integration cite
the need for political decisions to bring about economic integration, but they do not refer to political integration.   There obviously is an important
political aspect to Latin America's integration movement, but this is for the future.   The motive behind

United States support for this integration movement
is thus primarily to promote economic growth; in the
case of the European integration movement, the United States support was based primarily on the desire
to promote political unity. It has thus been easier
for the United States to support the free-trade area
of Latin America, while always maintaining some mis-
givings about the free-trade area in Europe. The
latter is a form of trade preferences among developed
countries; the former is trade preferences among less-
developed ones. Both are regional and the political
content is not necessarily greater in the less-
developed-country case--but the ideas of social jus-
tice and economic improvement pervade regional less-
developed preferences.

From time to time there has been doubt among
some Latin Americans that the United States supported
their integration movements, particularly before
President Kennedy. This skepticism may be greatest
when the United States Government exerts pressure on
behalf of certain exporters, for example, as was done
for sulphur and rosin exporters in 1963 and 1964 who
alleged they were losing Latin American markets as
the result of intra-LAFTA nontariff preferences.
The United States opposition on monopoly grounds to
the CACM integration-industry concept sometimes has
been interpreted as opposition to the integration
movement itself. However, the record of United
States support of the Latin American integration
movement was clear, even before President Kennedy
and Punta del Este. For example, President Eisenhower commented in 1960 following a two-week trip to
Latin America:

> we are encouraged by the progress being
> made toward the creation of common mar-
> kets. Large areas, relatively free of
> trade restrictions, will make for great-
> er efficiency in production and distri-
> bution and will attract new capital to
> speed development.[28]

PROBLEMS OF INTEGRATION AMONG
LESS-DEVELOPED COUNTRIES

Customs union problems are different for rich
and poor countries in several significant respects.
The most important difference relates to the polarization effects which frequently accompany development and the inability of poor countries to handle
this problem through financial means in the way that
the EEC is attempting to deal with it. Another important difference, and this has become particularly
significant in the LAFTA context, is the greater
apparent resistance to competition by entrepreneurs
in less-developed countries than in the more developed ones. This statement is not intended as an absolute; competition is accepted in both kinds of
countries, and is resisted in both kinds. But
wealthier market economies have some tradition of
competition and poorer ones generally have not.

Dell has argued that competition does not necessarily foster greater efficiency than monopoly.[29]
This may or may not be true. But in the present context the point is that businessmen in regional groupings of developed countries are willing to meet some
competition from businessmen in other countries of
the grouping; businessmen within regional groupings
of less-developed countries not only want protection
from nonmember-country imports, but also want protection against other member countries. Dell makes
this point: "And we should frankly recognize that
one of the principal aims of a common market for underdeveloped countries must be to broaden the scope
and increase the efficiency of protection, and not
to break it down."[30] Resistance to competition from
within the regional grouping has led in LAFTA, to
cite one case, to strong resistance against automatic
and across-the-board reductions in tariffs for trade
internally; instead there are annual negotiated reductions. By merely having a formula for an annual
percentage tariff reduction, the LAFTA model thereby
permits countries to pick and choose the easy reductions first, and not have to face the tariff reductions on sensitive items until later.

These annual negotiations and selective tariff
reductions within LAFTA obviously are cumbersome.
The system does force the reopening each year of decisions which had to be taken only once in the EEC
and EFTA, which use across-the-board and automatic
annual reductions. Distinguished Latin Americans
have from time to time called for a more automatic
system.[31]   It is of some significance, however, that
these calls do not normally come from the responsible
political or business leaders of the LAFTA countries,
but from the international bureaucrats. The issue
is not merely a technical one, but also touches on
business psychology in less-developed countries.
Automaticity of reduction of internal tariff and nontariff barriers obviously is closely tied to the
polarization issue.

Viner's discussion of trade creation (purchas-
ing from a partner country rather than using higher
cost domestic production) and trade diversion (pur-
chasing from a partner country rather than from some
lower cost third country) has become the starting
point for most subsequent examination of customs
union questions.[32]   In an important sense, however,
the issue of trade diversion versus trade creation
is not one which most less-developed countries consider terribly vital. In a policy sense, they are
more interested in the distribution of industry.
Harry Johnson has in part addressed this point in
his emphasis of the importance of industrial production as an influence on government policy.[33]   Similarly, it is addressed in two articles by Cooper and
Massell.[34]

It is this industrial aspect, and the distribution among member countries of whatever gains there
may be from a common market, which is a critical element in the minds of policy makers in underdeveloped
countries.[35]

Myrdal and Hirschman both have dealt with this
subject, what Myrdal has called the spread effect
and Hirshman the polarization effect.[36]   Myrdal has
argued that what he calls circular causation "should
be the main hypothesis when studying economic under-

development and development."[37]   Myrdal's point is
that "the play of the forces in the market normally
tends to increase, rather than to decrease, the inequality between regions."[38]   Hirschman's discussion
of regional inequalities within a nation, or between
nations, is less dogmatic than Myrdal's and less
pessimistic since he points out that there have been
turning points after North-South (rich-poor) polarization has proceeded for a while. Williamson's empirical study of regional inequalities within a nation concluded that early stages of national development generated increasingly large North-South income
differentials, but that these tended to diminish
over time when convergence between regions became
more the rule.[39]   Williamson's conclusion is essentially the same as that reached in studies of the
Economic Commission for Europe and cited by Myrdal,
that the income disparities between regions have
been diminishing in the richer countries and widening in the poorer ones.[40]

Dell has particularized this polarization problem both to Latin America and to regional economic
groupings of poor countries in general.[41]   The customs union case is comparable to the single country
regional disparity case since a group of countries
in a single common market have no internal trade
barriers; and in a sense the issue is even more complex in a customs union since, while no trade barriers
may exist, barriers to factor movements, particularly
labor, usually do continue. Dell has stated the customs union polarization issue in the following terms:

> The basic difficulty lies in the ten-
> dency of new enterprise to gravitate to
> those areas where an industrial base
> with all the requisite facilities al-
> ready exists. But the problem has
> been intensified by a system under which
> the poorer areas are compelled to buy
> high-cost manufactures from the richer
> areas--thus, in effect, subsidizing their
> industries. . . .[42]

The polarization issue is an important one in

Latin America. It is really the central issue raised
in the proposals of the four distinguished Latin
Americans (Herrera, Sanz de Santamaría, Mayobre, and
Prebisch) for a Latin American common market. It is
the issue which the complementation industry idea of
LAFTA and the integrated industry idea of the CACM
(neither of which has worked terribly well) try to
solve. And it is the issue which makes political
leaders reluctant to accept automatic and general
tariff reductions within a Latin American common market. What the political leaders of the poorer Latin
American countries fear is that in a common market,
with free internal movement of goods, the industrial
investment would move to the countries where the
infrastructure, the trained workmen, and the entrepreneurs, already exist, i.e., away from their countries.

Latin American industry developed by what
Prebisch called "inward-looking industrialization,"
using import substitution and high protection.
Prebisch and others have pointed out that the easy
phase of import substitution has passed in Latin
America.[43] Regional integration of Latin America is
a technique for widening the scope for import substitution. To the extent that this greater import substitution, covering a number of countries rather than
a single country, is high cost due to excessive protection, this further complicates the cost of polarization for the poorer countries of the region. The
poor countries which would not get much of the new
industrial investment, but which would be within the
new high tariff area protecting the industry, would,
as Dell noted, be helping to subsidize the richer
countries.

LAFTA has a series of ideas to try to meet this
problem. One LAFTA principle is reciprocity, that
each country gets in benefits as much as it gives in
costs. LAFTA's tariff policy is one instrument to
help assure reciprocity. The tariff reciprocity
works on a system of special preferences to the less-
developed of the LAFTA countries, i.e., Paraguay and
Ecuador;[44] to date, the preferences do not seem to
have been very important.

But the key technique for solving the polarization issue is intended to be investment planning.
The LAFTA complementarity idea is to set up different parts of large industries in different countries,
on less than a full regional basis, e.g., Chile
might make those parts of an automobile needing copper, Brazil might have the assembly plants, Argentina
might manufacture engines, etc. The concept has not
really worked to date. One recent study of LAFTA
noted: "The history of private enterprise complementarity agreements to date is hardly encouraging even
to the most optimistic of the integracionistas."[45]
There are two such agreements in existence, for data
processing equipment and radio tubes.

The LAFTA complementarity and the CACM integrated industry ideas are interesting efforts to com-
bine preferential trade within a region with investment policy in the same region. Under both programs,
investment in certain industries will be accompanied
by trade preferences for that industry. Even though
these particular programs have been less than fully
successful to date, the concept of combining investment and preferences deserves careful study.

In their recent paper, the four Latin American
economic experts proposed something more bold than
complementarity, "to plan the development of these
industries on a regional scale"; they cited iron and
steel, some nonferrous metals, some groups of heavy
chemical and petro-chemical industries including fertilizers, and the manufacture of motor vehicles,
ships, and heavy industrial equipment. These are industries in which they believed economies of scale
exist. This is an ambitious concept. It would involve continental industrial planning and planned
allocation of industries on a country-by-country
basis. To avoid polarization, parts of complex industries, or complete simple industries, would have
to go to less- as well as to more-developed of the
LAFTA countries. The idea of planning what country
gets what part of what industry (this is different
from planning for such regional facilities as transportation and communications which must be located
in all the countries) is precisely what the Russian-

sponsored Council for Mutual Economic Assistance
(CEMA or Comecon) tried to do and failed.

The proposals of Herrera-Sanz de Santamaría-
Mayobre-Prebisch grew out of a letter of January 6,
1965, from President Eduardo Frei of Chile; the
Chileans had been advocating greater supranationality
in the Latin American integration movement. In order
to carry out industrial planning for a continent, and
to decide which country gets which part of which industry, some degree of supranationality would be required. The proposal of the four envisaged a Council of Ministers and argued "that the right to veto
the Council's decisions should be restricted from
the outset."[46] This has not been accepted as the
political level of governments.

This detail on polarization, and the efforts to
solve the problem in a Latin American preferential
grouping, has been given in order to highlight the
crucial nature of this issue for policy-makers in
less-developed countries. Whether polarization is
likely to be as serious as Myrdal implies, or whether
it is a problem more easily solved, is less important
in a policy sense than the fact that political leaders of any country must be able to produce benefits
for their country, as well as pay costs, from a regional integration scheme; they must be able to demonstrate "reciprocity," to use the LAFTA word. The
problem is not unique to LAFTA; it probably was even
more serious in the earlier East African Common Market of Kenya, Uganda, and Tanganyika, in which the
gains went primarily to Kenya.[47]

What is important to keep in mind in trying to
understand the gyrations of policy-makers in less-
developed countries is that this is not a simple
issue for them. It may be a solvable problem, but
not by sloganeering or ringing declarations.[48] The
politicians in Latin America may not be all wrong in
moving ahead cautiously toward a common market.
Trade preferences among developing countries are not
a panacea. And, in point of fact, LAFTA has not yet
been the failure its critics aver; in January, 1966,
LAFTA completed its fifth round of tariff reductions

and the negotiations are beginning to get into the
more difficult items, such as semiprocessed goods.
The test for LAFTA will come in the next few years,
when further tariff cuts will have to affect the
hard items; it will be time enough then to judge
LAFTA's effectiveness.

CONCLUDING COMMENTS ON PREFERENCES
AMONG DEVELOPING COUNTRIES

Some industries, like pigs, are more industrial
than others. Fertilizer and iron and steel and
motor vehicles--some of the industries cited by
Herrera-Sanz de Santamaría-Mayobre-Prebisch on which
total Latin American planning is suggested--are
among the industries where scale is of some significance. It is precisely for these industries that
preferences among developing countries--usually in
the form of some regional arrangement both because
of the economies of transport for such industries as
fertilizers permitted by regionalism and also because a regional arrangement permits the appropriate
institutional and political decisions to be made--
holds great promise.

There are other types of industries--small
machinery, clothing, bicycles, toys, and literally
thousands of others--where there probably is no high
correlation between scale and efficiency. Preferences among developing countries also could help for
these industries, for which the national market concept of Rostow seems highly relevant. But these are
not normally the large-scale enterprises that the
Latin American planners seem to have in mind when
they talk of industrialization.

There obviously is place in less-developed countries for both types of industries. As Bauer and
Yamey have pointed out: "In the conditions prevailing in many under-developed countries the development
of small industry may be the most economic form of
industrialization; it may be more economic than
either large-scale organized industry or cottage industry."[49] In other cases, such as for steel in

India, or larger plants in place of the present host
of small plants for the automobile industry in Latin
America, large-scale plants are desirable. The institutional conditions, and degree of planning, the
extent of supranational political control required
within a customs or economic union, differ for the
different types of industries.

President Johnson has indicated United States
support for certain regional industries in Latin
America; both he and Herrera-Sanz de Santamaría-
Mayobre-Prebisch cited fertilizers. How can the
United States help? With money (resources) and tech-
nicians, probably; and also with understanding that
it is not easy to set up a protected fertilizer industry in, say, Brazil and then ask Argentina to buy
that fertilizer if it costs more than fertilizer ob-
tainable elsewhere--unless Argentina gets something
in return. What is true for Brazil and Argentina in
this hypothetical case of fertilizer cuts across all
countries, particularly the poorer ones, in Latin
America, in any common market among them.

It is for this reason, principally, that the
political leaders in the Latin American countries
have been and are moving cautiously toward a Latin
American common market which would have all the
trappings of supranationality, including centralized
political leadership for economic decisions over
which no country could impose a veto. Each integration movement must move at its own pace, whether
this is for European political integration or Latin
American or African economic integration. In this
sense, the responsible political leaders who must
answer to some constituency probably know better
what is possible than do the international bureaucrats who insist on getting the whole hog now rather
than achieving something now and more later. Viewed
in this perspective, LAFTA and the Latin American integration movement as a whole has been far more successful than its critics would admit; it has not yet
achieved the whole hog, but the forward momentum to
economic integration is being maintained thus far.

The discussion has mentioned but not focused on

regional payments arrangements among developing countries. These would not be easy to devise, particularly in Latin America where currencies are mostly
convertible and where some countries are constant
debtors and may have to be financed by other poor
countries. And in general, the Latin American central bankers themselves have preferred to proceed
cautiously. At the same time, it must be recognized
that a payments union among developing countries,
all of which may have overvalued exchange rates,
could facilitate preferential exports among themselves for products which could not be exported on
world markets because of the exchange rates. This
is not intended to be an argument either for or
against regional payments unions among developing
countries as a device to preferentially promote
their trade, but rather only to note that the issue
is one of some interest which requires attention.

The discussion also has mentioned quotas and
other nontariff devices, as opposed to tariffs, as a
possible technique to implement regional preferences.
To a degree, LAFTA already has done this by adding
surcharges on top of tariff duties and then forgiv-
ing the surcharges only for members of the free-trade
area. (It also is possible under both general and
selective systems of preferences by developed to
less-developed countries to effect the preferences
through quota or other nontariff devices rather than
through tariffs, although this suggestion has not
yet been advocated forcefully by developing country
spokesmen.) The use of nontariff preference techniques, particularly in regional arrangements of developing countries, may or may not be desirable in
promoting economic development, but it clearly is
another issue which deserves deeper study.

These possibilities of regional payments unions
and regional nontariff preferences, like the issue
of regional industries, are other arguments in favor
of regionalism in preferential trade among developing countries and against ad hoc preferences between
any pair of developing countries without regard to
region. The political decisions permitting greater
supranationality in economic decision-making in

Latin America, or in Africa, cannot   now be taken;
but by keeping preferences on a regional basis, the
possibility to make these political decisions in the
future will not be compromised.

United States policy should promote such regionalism with resources and understanding, where possible;
and it should resist intra-developing-country preferences which would tend to frustrate this kind of
regionalism.

Notes to Chapter 6

1. Article XVIII, Paragraph 1 of the GATT has
a definition of a less-developed country, which is
imprecise but has served its purpose thus far:
"contracting parties the economies of which can only
support low standards of living and are in the early
stages of development." BISD, Vol. I (revised),
April, 1955, p. 34.

2. Article XXIV, Paragraph 8(a)(i). Emphasis
supplied.

3. Towards a New Trade Policy for Development,
Report by the Secretary-General of the United Nations
Conference on Trade and Development, United Nations,
New York, 1964, pp. 38-39.

4. New Zealand's Trade with Australia, Presented
to the House of Representatives by Leave (By Authority:
R. E. Owen, Government Printer, Wellington, New Zealand, 1965), p. 14.

5. Clair Wilcox, A Charter for World Trade (New
York: Macmillan, 1949), p. 70.

6. Isaiah Frank, The European Common Market
(New York: Frederick A. Praeger, 1961).

7. Sidney Dell, Trade Blocs and Common Markets
(New York: Alfred A. Knopf, 1963).

8. Jacob Viner, The Customs Union Issue (New York: Carnegie Endowment for International Peace, 1950), p. 49.

9. The quotation is from Anthony M. Solomon, Assistant Secretary of State for Economic Affairs, in Latin American Development and Western Hemisphere Trade, Hearings before the Subcommittee on Inter-American Relationships of the Joint Economic Commit-tee of the United States Congress, September 8-10, 1965, p. 151.

10. Ibid., p. 209.

11. The Coal-Steel Community is fully and ex-cellently discussed in William Diebold, Jr., The Schuman Plan (New York: Frederick A. Praeger, 1959).

12. BISD, Third Supplement, p. 208.

13. U.S. Department of State, "Havana Charter for an International Trade Organization," publica-tion 3206, March 24, 1948. Released September, 1948.

14. UNCTAD, Geneva, March 23-June 16, 1964, Final Act with Related Documents (London: Her Majes-ty's Stationery Office, July, 1964, Cmnd. 2417), pp. 176-77.

15. These latter are suggestions contained in UNCTAD document E/CONF.46/74, February 27, 1964, Memorandum Concerning Certain Items on the Agenda of the United Nations Conference on Trade and Develop-ment, submitted by France, Paragraphs 74 ff.

16. Viner, op. cit., p. 49.

17. Ibid., p. 41.

18. Some of the Post editorials critical of the agreement were on January 17, September 22, Sep-tember 30, and October 4, all 1965. The following is from the September 22, 1965, editorial: "In Janu-ary President Johnson and Prime Minister Pearson of Canada signed an agreement that was widely heralded

as a measure to establish 'free trade' in automobiles between the two countries. In later releases
the term 'freer trade' was substituted. And now,
with House hearings completed some time ago and a
parade of witnesses still appearing before the Senate Finance Committee, the public is learning that
words do not always mean what one wants them to
mean."

19. The U.K.-EEC negotiations are thoroughly discussed in Miriam Camps, Britain and the European Community, 1955-1963 (Princeton, N.J.: Princeton University Press, 1964).

20. Viner, op. cit., p. 95.

21. R. T. Nichols, The Common Market and European Unification (Santa Monica, California: The
RAND Corporation, 1965), p. 100.

22. Bela Balassa, "European Integration: Problems and Issues," American Economic Review, LIII, No.
2 (May, 1963), 175-84.

23. Alexander Lamfalussy, "Europe's Progress:
Due to Common Market?" Lloyds Bank Review (October,
1961), pp. 1-16. Quotation cited from p. 1.

24. One example of this is Dexter M. Keezer
and associates, New Forces in American Business (New
York: McGraw-Hill Book Company, 1959).

25. And there seems to be no end of books and
pamphlets on the EEC. Some which might be cited are
Emile Benoit, Europe at Sixes and Sevens (New York:
Columbia University Press, 1961); The European Markets, A Guide for American Businessmen, Chase Manhattan Bank, January, 1964; J. F. Deniau, The Common
Market (London: Barrie and Rockliff, 1962); Frank,
op. cit.; Randall Hinshaw, The European Community
and American Trade (paperback; New York: Frederick
A. Praeger, 1964); Don D. Humphrey, The United States
and the Common Market (New York: Frederick A.
Praeger, 1962); Finn B. Jensen and Ingo Walter, The
Common Market: Economic Integration in Europe

(Philadelphia: Lippincott & Co., 1965); and literally hundreds of shorter articles.

26. The quotations are from <u>Proposals for the
Creation of the Latin American Common Market</u>, Trade
and Development Board document TD/B/11, April 15,
1965. The authors of the document are four distinguished Latin Americans: Felipe Herrera, President of the Inter-American Development Bank; Carlos
Sanz de Santamaría, Chairman of the Inter-American
Committee for the Alliance for Progress; José An-
tonio Mayobre, Executive Secretary of the Economic
Commission for Latin America; and Raúl Prebisch,
Secretary-General of UNCTAD. The document will hereafter be referred to as <u>Proposals</u>.

27. From the Charter of Punta del Este establishing an Alliance for Progress, August 17, 1961.

28. Report to the nation, March 8, 1960, <u>De-
partment of State Bulletin</u>, XLII, No. 1083 (March
28, 1960), 473. Other important statements supporting Latin American integration were made by R. R.
Rubottom, Jr., Assistant Secretary of State for Inter-
American Affairs, April 9, 1960, DOSB, May 2, 1960,
p. 697; Douglas Dillon, Under Secretary of State,
DOSB, March 21, 1960; and President Kennedy on March
13, 1961, on the Alliance for Progress, DOSB, April
3, 1961, p. 473.

29. Dell, <u>op. cit.</u>, p. 217.

30. <u>Ibid</u>.

31. This call is reiterated in <u>Proposals</u>, <u>op.
cit.</u>, pp. 12-14.

32. Viner, <u>op. cit.</u>

33. Harry G. Johnson, "An Economic Theory of
Protectionism, Tariff Bargaining, and the Formation
of Customs Unions," <u>The Journal of Political Economy</u>,
LXXIII, No. 3 (June, 1965), 256-83.

34. C. A. Cooper and B. F. Massell, "Toward a
General Theory of Customs Unions for Developing Countries" and "A New Look at Customs Union Theory," The
RAND Corporation, September and November, 1964. The
first article has appeared in The Journal of Political Economy, LXXIII, No. 5 (October, 1965), 461-76.

35. Some other important works not thus far
cited on customs union theory include James E. Meade,
The Theory of Customs Unions (Amsterdam: North-
Holland Publishing Co., 1955); Richard G. Lipsey,
"Trade Diversion and Welfare," Economica, XXIV (Feb-
ruary, 1957), 40-46, and "The Theory of Customs
Unions: A General Survey," Economic Journal, LXX
(September, 1960), 496-513; and Bela Balassa, The
Theory of Economic Integration (Homewood, Illinois:
Richard D. Irwin, Inc., 1961).

36. The relevant works are Gunnar Myrdal, Rich
Lands and Poor: The Road to World Prosperity (New
York: Harper & Brothers, 1957); and Albert O.
Hirschman, The Strategy of Economic Development
(paperback; New Haven: Yale University Press, 1958).

37. Ibid., p. 23.

38. Ibid., p. 27.

39. Jeffrey G. Williamson, "Regional Inequality and the Process of National Development: A
Description of the Patterns," Economic Development
and Cultural Change, XIII, No. 4, Part II (July,
1965).

40. Myrdal, op. cit., pp. 33-34, cited from
the Economic Surveys of Europe of 1954 and 1955.

41. The Latin American case is discussed in
Sidney Dell, Problemas de un mercado común en América
Latina (México, D. F.: Centro de Estudios Monetarios
Latinoamericanos, 1959); and the more general case in
Dell, op. cit., to which further reference will be
made.

42. Dell, op. cit., p. 239.

43.   See discussion in Towards a New Trade Policy for Development, op. cit., pp. 20 ff. This policy of highly protected, inward-looking industrialization was one stimulated in part by ECLA economists.

44.   These special tariff concessions are given by the seven more advanced countries, Argentina, Brazil, Colombia, Chile, Mexico, Peru, and Uruguay, on an item-by-item negotiated basis. They are published; for example in the case of Paraguay, see ALALC (Asociacion Latinoamericana de Libre Comercio), "Lista de ventajas no extensivas otorgadas a Paraguay (Articulo 32, inc. a), 1965."

45.   Ernest B. Haas and Philippe C. Schmitter, The Politics of Economics in Latin American Regionalism: The Latin American Free Trade Association after Four Years of Operation, Monograph No. 2, 1965-66 (The Social Science Foundation and the Graduate School of International Studies, University of Denver), p. 25.

46.   Proposals, op. cit., p. 27.

47.   See Benton F. Massell, The Distribution of Gains in a Common Market: the East African Case (Santa Monica, California: The RAND Corporation, 1964).

48.   Among the writers who tend to treat glibly of automaticity of tariff reductions in a Latin American common market, or who simplify the issue of the distribution of gains, are Victor L. Urquidi, Free Trade and Economic Integration in Latin America (paperback; Berkeley: University of California Press, 1962); and Peter Nehemkis, Latin America, Myth and Reality (New York: Alfred A. Knopf, 1964).

49.   Peter T. Bauer and Basil S. Yamey, The Economics of Under-Developed Countries (Chicago: The University of Chicago Press, 1957), p. 253.

CHAPTER **7** CONCLUSIONS

This has been a study of only one aspect of
United States trade policy toward less-developed
countries. It has dealt primarily with exports of
manufactured and processed goods from the poor nations. Therefore, it has omitted for the most part
such key but related issues as trade in primary products, the development of synthetics, the scope for
trade between the poor countries and the Communist
countries, the burgeoning debt burden of the poor
countries, the quantity and terms of future aid, population problems, the role of social and educational
and political factors in economic development.

Still, despite omissions, this has been a discussion of development, and the role of trade in the
process of development. George Woods, the President
of IBRD, recently set forth some income parameters
of the development problem.[1]

The figures, imprecise though they may be, do
give the order of magnitude of the disparity in incomes between the rich and poor countries. The central issue really is less one of reducing income disparities, important as this is psychologically in an
age of rapid communication, as it is one of raising the
incomes of the poorer thousands of millions of people
on earth. In the process of the poor becoming richer,
there is no reason why the richer should not become
even more wealthy. Trade has a role in this process;
and that is what the preference issue is all about.

TABLE 11

Annual Per Capita Incomes
(Value figures in U.S. dollars)

	Amount	Millions of People
Very poor	Less than $100	990
Poor	$100 to $250	1,150
Middle income	$250 to $750	390
High income	More than $750	810
EEC	$1,400	175
United States	$3,000	194

Source: Foreign Affairs, XLIV, No. 2 (January,
         1966), 206.

The purpose of this final chapter is to summar-
ize conclusions about the preference issue which
have emerged from the previous analytical discussion.
The following--keeping in mind that the issue is
trade and development, and not just trade--are the
main conclusions.

1. The way things are done, as well as what is
done, counts. This, perhaps, was a problem at the
first UNCTAD for the United States, since many post-
UNCTAD comments were to the effect that the United
States stood rigidly on principle and adamantly and
isolatedly said "no." Since UNCTAD, the United
States really has not altered its position on preferences, but it has more clearly demonstrated its willingness to examine the issue.

Latin Americans sometimes date recent United
States interest in them to President Kennedy and the
Alliance for Progress. They frequently use the word
"mystique" or "charisma" to describe President
Kennedy's attraction in Latin America.[2] Those

familiar with United States trade policy toward
Latin America, however, know that President Eisenhower similarly supported Latin American economic
integration, and that United States unyielding opposition to commodity agreements shifted not after
President Kennedy assumed office, but during the latter days of the Eisenhower administration.

But, having said this, the reason that Presidents Kennedy and Roosevelt evoke a "good" reaction
in Latin America is because of the way they did
things, not merely what they did.

This is an important conclusion to keep in mind
in dealing with less-developed, frequently newly
independent, countries. They do not wish to be patronized; they seek development as a matter of twentieth century right and not of largesse from the
rich countries; they undoubtedly resent being lec-
tured to as little children. Style does count, in
the preference as in other issues.

2. Despite the language of the UNCTAD recommendation dealing with this subject, namely, that some
developed countries are opposed to the "principle" of
preferences,[3] the issue really is not one of principle. Isaiah Frank has raised this point:

> The fact that trade discrimination
> against outsiders is at the core of the
> moves toward economic regionalism
> raises the whole question of the rela-
> tionship and compatibility of these new
> developments with the basic multilateral
> principles of commercial policy that the
> United States has been espousing at
> least since the end of World War II.[4]

The "principle" per se becomes ludicrous as the ob-
ject of the preference battle when preferences have
been condoned over and over again: in the EEC, EFTA,
the ECSC, the Commonwealth, the EEC association
agreements, the United States-Canada automotive
agreement, and others. It is hard to argue, as some
have done, that the ECSC preferences were good be-

cause they were based on the political consideration
of unifying Europe, but that preferences for less-
developed countries based on economic development
grounds are not good.

During the meeting of the special committee on
preferences, it was argued that preferences would be
of little value to developing countries since they
still could not compete with domestic industries in
the three main markets, namely the EEC, EFTA, and
the United States.[5] The argument may be valid; but
it ignores the fact that intra-EEC and intra-EFTA
trade is preferential. And if these preferences
among developed countries are permissible ("legal"
so to speak, if one believes they conform with the
provisions of Article XXIV of the GATT), why not
preferences by them to less-developed countries?

It is not the principle which is at stake; it
is the most-favored-nation practice, and the reason
for international adoption of this practice and the
rigid safeguards countries acting in their collective capacities have attempted to put on countries
acting individually in departing from this practice.
What is relevant, as was stated at the outset of
this study, is the benefit to be gained from preferences as contrasted with the cost of departing from
the most-favored-nation concept (or principle,
viewed in this sense).

This may be a matter of style, and the standing
on principle may be a shorthand way of stating all
the things that lie behind the principle. The conclusion may be that it would be useful to alter the
style; but in any event, the United States should
deal with the preference issue pragmatically.

The issue of principle also cuts in the opposite direction. At the first UNCTAD, and since, developing country proponents of preferences have
argued that the first step is to accept the "principle" of preferences, and then to worry later about
the details, or even what "preferences" mean. As already has been discussed at some length, all preferences are not the same. It would be a mistake for

the United States to accept this position; there is
little merit in buying a pig-in-a-poke called preferences and then later trying to figure out what has
been bought.[6]

3.   Despite some belief that the reason the
United States opposes preferences is because the
United States is protectionist and wants to keep imports out, particularly imports from low-wage countries, it really is hard to see that the United
States would be immediately hurt by preferences.
This statement extracts from the ultimate possible
consequences on the United States of a possibly dis-
rupted world trade pattern resulting from preferences. The United States is a powerful and independent country and it could protect itself, if it felt
this were necessary. The issue, therefore, is
whether the United States and other developed countries would use preferences as a technique for over-
protecting; and there are indications that they would.

Another even more important reason for not looking at potential immediate trade damage to the United
States is that increased foreign-exchange earnings by
developing countries will result in greater imports
by them. Some developing countries do amass reserves
that are not spent, but not too many. And the evidence seems to be that the marginal propensity to import of developing countries due to greater foreign-
exchange earnings tends to result in a greater proportion of their imports from the United States than
does their average propensity to import.[7]

Thus, if some day the United States decided to
alter its preference position, the immediate danger
points to look for are the adverse effects on developing and borderline countries, not on the United
States--or even on other developed countries, which
for the most part could also protect themselves.

4.   The main substantive conclusion regarding
both general and selective preferences from developed
to less-developed countries is that the United States
should seek to provide itself with some legislative
flexibility.

The Trade Expansion Act of 1962 expired July 1, 1967, and either successor or amended legislation will be required. Obviously, the nature of the new legislation will be determined by the mood of the country at the time the legislation is under consideration; and this in turn will depend on a variety of factors such as the degree of prosperity or stagnation in the United States economy, the relative success or failure of the Kennedy round of trade negotiations, the proliferation (if any) of preferential arrangements between other developed and less-developed countries, and others. In any event, some legislation will be needed; it can be as or more liberal than the Trade Expansion Act, in a freer trade sense, if the conditions are favorable, and it may be considerably more protectionist if the reverse is the case.

The kind of flexibility suggested is to permit the United States to roll with the punches of events. In addition, the United States trade legislation should take more explicit and more meaningful recognition of the trade problems of the developing countries. The developing countries' needs are touched on in the Trade Expansion Act of 1962 (essentially in Section 213 dealing with tropical agricultural and forestry commodities[8]), but not in any significant way.

The following are among the kinds of flexibility and recognition of developing-country interests that might be considered:

At a minimum, the legislation should look to reducing or eliminating the escalation in tariffs as the degree of processing increases.

The legislation might, more significantly, look to future negotiations among the world's industrialized countries for duty-free treatment, to be reached in stages over, say, ten to fifteen years, and to provide this same duty-free treatment for most manufactured products at once for less-developed countries. As noted in earlier discussion, this may not be politically practicable, but it is worth a try,

both because of its efficiency advantages for the developed countries and because it would minimize the
potential costs of preferences for developing countries.

In order to try to eliminate reverse preferences
that less-developed countries now give on a reciprocal basis to developed countries, i.e., to attempt
to return to some form of open-door system, any United States legislation of the foregoing type should
give the President the option to refuse preferences
to any less-developed country which discriminates in
its import policy against the United States. Less-
developed countries generally do not give preferences
to developed nations because they want to, but rather
because they are pressured into doing so; and the
less-developed countries might even welcome some
pressure from the United States to permit them to import goods from the cheapest world sources.

While it does not now seem desirable, the United
States may as a defensive step wish itself to enter
into selective preferences, particularly on a regional basis with Latin America, and this contingency
should be provided for.

5. The institution by the United States of any
preference system would have costs. The following
are illustrative of these. Under a general system,
these costs would be reflected in aid allocations,
probable increased import restrictions of various
kinds in the United States, damage to borderline
countries defined as "developed," greater difficulty
in reducing most-favored-nation rates. These are
considerations which cannot be ignored if there is
sincerity on the part of the United States in wanting
to help less-developed countries in their development;
they can be ignored if there is merely a desire to
maneuver for position to temporarily win some plaudits
from developing countries, or to embarrass other developed countries.

Under a selective system, excluded countries
could be hurt. And, under a selective system, the
establishment of spheres-of-influence could have
profound costs which cannot be ignored.

The conclusion following from this important consideration is that preferences probably are not desirable but, if instituted, should be done in some fashion so as to minimize the potential magnitude of these costs.

6.   There are other potential techniques for assisting development through some trade tie, and these too should be examined in preparing for the next United States legislation. Some of these--such as regional payments unions among developing countries, currency devaluations by developing countries, export subsidies for trade in manufactured goods, seeking better techniques for tying investment and preferences--have been cited briefly in the discussion. Other related techniques, which have not been discussed, may be worth noting at this point.

One such technique with some promise which has been suggested by some is that the developed countries might set up targets for imports from developing countries,[9] breaking the targets down by both primary and manufactured goods. Given the free-enterprise nature of the United States, it probably would not be practical to make this target an obligation (with some financial penalty or increase in aid if it is not met); but a target, with a solemn indication of sincere effort to live up to it, has meaning in and of itself. The meaning would be enhanced if all developed countries undertook similar targets, perhaps coordinated in the OECD, and if the developed countries then subjected themselves to confrontation and suggestions for remedial action if the targets were not met.

Another technique suggested by some is for developed countries to rebate to developing countries import duties collected on products of the latter.[10] A tariff preference on a manufactured good may benefit particular producers, exporters, or sectors, but the ultimate general benefit to the economy as a whole will depend on how the particular benefits are used. To many, this is a point of strength of the tariff preference technique, since its success will depend on the initiative of entrepreneurs.[11] However,

there also is scope for the provision of financial
assistance to less-developed economies as a whole,
or to pinpointed sectors of these economies, and the
rebate of import duties collected could be so used.

Viewed from the vantage of the United States,
where the rebate of any import duty collected would
have to go through the appropriation mechanism of
the Congress, this technique is merely another device for appropriating foreign aid. If the rebates
were to go back to the exporting country itself, it
would be a form of preferential treatment for exports. If the rebates were to go to developing countries as a whole, without regard to the particular
countries whose exports generated the import duty receipts, then the technique really has no advantage
over present aid appropriation procedures. The rebate suggestion also has the potential disadvantage
that it could encourage developed countries to maintain relatively high import tariffs, and thereby restrict trade, on the grounds that the duties collected are being returned in any event to the developing countries.

The conclusion is that the rebate suggestion
deserves study--probably more for primary commodities than for manufactured goods since the elasticities of demand may be less for the former than the
latter and the duties may do less harm in impeding
consumption--but that maintaining duties merely as a
device to be able to provide aid seems like a retro-
grade step since aid can be provided through other
appropriation techniques without impeding total
trade flows.

7. The United States should also encourage
regional preferences, and regional economic integration, among developing countries. By "encouragement"
is meant the provision of resources where these are
necessary and the demonstration of some understanding
of the difficulties. This is an area of greater potential for most developing countries than preferences from developed countries.

In concluding these final comments, it may
be useful to reiterate: The policy alternatives for
the United States in dealing with the preference
issue relate both to style and substance, and both
are important; and the substance is not merely a matter of trade, as important as that is, but of development and of the world economic and political order.

Notes to Chapter 7

1.   In an article "The Development Decade in
the Balance," Foreign Affairs, XLIV, No. 2 (January,
1966), 206-15. The figures given are from this
article.

2.   I can cite many Latin Americans to document
this point; indeed, I am almost directly quoting
Carlos Sanz de Santamaría about President Kennedy's
"mystique," and about the Latin American feeling
that Franklin Roosevelt cared about Western Hemisphere relations and then that no subsequent United
States President really did until Kennedy.

3.   UNCTAD, Final Act, Annex A.III.5.

4.   Isaiah Frank, The European Common Market
(New York: Frederick A. Praeger, 1961), p. 2.

5.   Report of the Special Committee on Preferences, TD/B/C.2/1 and TD/B/AC.1/4, June 4, 1965,
Paragraph 12.

6.   The relevant phrase from Annex A.III.5 of
the Final Act of UNCTAD reads: "Noting that all the
developing countries and a great majority of the developed countries have signified their agreement with
the principle of assisting the industrial development
of the developing countries by the extension of preferences in their favour."

7.   This is a point called to my attention and
amply documented by John Pincus.

8.   Section 213 permits the United States to eliminate import duties and other restrictions on tropical agricultural and forestry products provided "the like article is not produced in significant quantities in the United States" and provided also that the EEC gives "comparable" access on a non-discriminatory basis. What this really does, at least as far as the United States is concerned, is to give away nothing provided somebody else does something; and its motivation seems more to secure EEC liberalization rather than to give any significant United States benefits.

9.   Various United States officials have suggested this in internal discussions. Within the academic community, Irving Kravis subsequently made the same suggestion during a meeting in 1965 to discuss trade problems of less-developed countries.

10.   France made this suggestion for dealing with imports of primary products, although the funds returned obviously could be used for various developmental purposes by the developing countries. See Memorandum Concerning Certain Items on the Agenda of the United Nations Conference on Trade and Development, submitted by France, document E/CONF.46/74, February 27, 1964, pp. 12 ff. Israel suggested that Committee III of the GATT "should give consideration to . . . the provision of export assistance funds by industrialized countries . . . derived from customs duty receipts on imports from less-developed countries. . . ." BISD, Twelfth Supplement (June, 1964), p. 123.

11.   Prebisch has made this point in Towards a New Trade Policy for Development, Report by the Secretary-General of the United Nations Conference on Trade and Development (New York: United Nations, 1964), p. 69.

BIBLIOGRAPHY

BIBLIOGRAPHY

Books

Avramovic, Dragoslav, et al. Economic Growth and External Debt. Baltimore: The Johns Hopkins Press, 1964.

Bailey, Thomas A. A Diplomatic History of the American People. Sixth edition. New York: D. Appleton and Co., 1958.

Balassa, Bela. The Theory of Economic Integration. Homewood, Illinois: Richard D. Irwin, Inc., 1961.

_____. Trade Prospects for Developing Countries. Homewood, Illinois: Richard D. Irwin, Inc., 1964.

Bauer, Peter T., and Basil S. Yamey. The Economics of Under-Developed Countries. Chicago: The University of Chicago Press, 1957.

Beer, George Louis. The Old Colonial System, 1660-1754. New York: The Macmillan Company, 1912.

Bemis, Samuel Flagg. A Diplomatic History of the United States. Fourth edition. New York: Holt, Rinehart and Winston, 1955.

_____. The Latin American Policy of the United States. New York: Harcourt, Brace and Co., 1943.

Benoit, Emile. Europe at Sixes and Sevens. New York: Columbia University Press, 1961.

Camps, Miriam. Britain and the European Community, 1955-1963. Princeton, N.J.: Princeton University Press, 1964.

213

Culbertson, William Smith. Commercial Policy in War
    Time and After. New York and London: D. Apple-
    ton and Co., 1924.

Curzon, Gerard. Multilateral Commercial Diplomacy:
    An Examination of the Impact of the General
    Agreement on Tariffs and Trade on National Com-
    mercial Policies and Techniques. London:
    Michael Joseph, 1965.

Davis, Hugh O. America's Trade Equality Policy.
    Washington, D.C.:   American Council on Public
    Affairs, 1942.

Dell, Sidney. Problemas de un mercado común en
    América Latina. México, D.F.:   Centro de
    Estudios Monetarios Latinoamericanos, 1959.

_____. Trade Blocs and Common Markets. New York:
    Alfred A. Knopf, 1963.

Deniau, J. F. The Common Market. London: Barrie
    and Rockliff, 1962.

Diebold, William, Jr. The Schuman Plan. New York:
    Frederick A. Praeger, Publishers, 1959.

Frank, Isaiah. The European Common Market. New
    York: Frederick A. Praeger, Publishers, 1961.

Gardner, Richard N. In Pursuit of World Order. New
    York: Frederick A. Praeger, Publishers, 1964.

Gregory, T. E. G. Tariffs: A Study in Method.
    London: Charles Griffin & Co., Ltd., 1921.

Haberler, Gottfried. The Theory of International
    Trade. New York: The Macmillan Company, 1936.

Hansen, Alvin H. The Dollar and the International
    Monetary System. New York: McGraw-Hill Book
    Co., 1965.

Herod, Joseph Rogers. Favored Nation Treatment:
    An Analysis of the Most Favored Nation Clause.
    New York: Banks Law Publishing Co., 1901.

Hinshaw, Randall. The European Community and
    American Trade. New York: Frederick A.
    Praeger, Publishers, 1964. (Paperback.)

Hirschman, Albert O. The Strategy of Economic
    Development. New Haven: Yale University
    Press, 1958. (Paperback.)

Humphrey, Don D. The United States and the Common
    Market. New York: Frederick A. Praeger,
    Publishers, 1962.

Jensen, Finn B., and Ingo Walter. The Common
    Market: Economic Integration in Europe.
    Philadelphia: Lippincott & Co., 1965.

Johnson, Harry G. U.S. Economic Policy Towards the
    Less-Developed Countries: A Survey of Major
    Issues. Washington, D.C.: The Brookings
    Institution, forthcoming.

_____, and Peter B. Kenen. Trade and Develop-
    ment. Geneva: Librairie Droz, 1965, pp. 9-29.

Johnson, Willis Fletcher. An American Statesman:
    The Works and Words of James G. Blaine.
    Augusta Publishing Co., 1892.

Keezer, Dexter M., and associates. New Forces in
    American Business. New York: McGraw-Hill
    Book Co., 1959.

Kindleberger, Charles P. Foreign Trade and the
    National Income. New Haven: Yale University
    Press, 1962. (Paperback.)

Maizels, Alfred. Industrial Growth and World Trade:
    An Empirical Study of Trends in Production,
    Consumption and Trade in Manufactures from
    1899-1959 with a Discussion of Probable Future
    Trends.   New York: Cambridge University
    Press, 1963.

Meade, James E. The Theory of Customs Unions.
    Amsterdam: North Holland Publishing Co., 1955.

Morison, Samuel Eliot. The Oxford History of the American People. New York: Oxford University Press, 1965.

Myrdal, Gunnar. An International Economy, Problems and Prospects. New York: Harper & Brothers, 1956.

_____. Challenge to Affluence. New York: Pantheon, 1962-63.

_____. Rich Lands and Poor: The Road to World Prosperity. New York: Harper & Brothers, 1957.

Nehemkis, Peter. Latin America, Myth and Reality. New York: Alfred A. Knopf, 1964.

North, Douglass C. The Economic Growth of the United States, 1790-1860. New York: Prentice-Hall, 1961.

Nurkse, Ragnar. Patterns of Trade and Development. Stockholm: Almquist & Wiksell, 1959.

Pincus, John. Economic Aid and International Cost Sharing. Santa Monica, California: The RAND Corporation, July, 1965. Also, Baltimore: The Johns Hopkins Press, 1965.

Powelson, John P. Latin America: Today's Economic and Social Revolution. New York: McGraw-Hill Book Co., 1964.

Reuber, Grant L. Canada's Interest in the Trade Problems of the Less-Developed Countries. Montreal: Private Planning Association of Canada, 1964.

Reuss, Henry S. The Critical Decade. New York: McGraw-Hill Book Co., 1964.

Robinson, E. A. G. (ed.). Economic Consequences of the Size of Nations. London: The Macmillan Company, 1960.

Rostow, W. W. The Stages of Economic Growth.
    New York: Cambridge University Press, 1960.
    (Paperback.)

Scitovsky, Tibor. Economic Theory and Western
    European Integration. Stanford: Stanford
    University Press, 1958.

Strackbein, O. R. American Enterprise and Foreign
    Trade. Washington, D.C.: Public Affairs
    Press, 1965.

Tasca, Henry J. The Reciprocal Trade Policy of the
    United States. Philadelphia: University of
    Pennsylvania Press, 1938.

Taussig, Frank William. The Tariff History of the
    United States. Eighth edition. New York:
    Putnam, 1931.

Urquidi, Victor L. Free Trade and Economic Integra-
    tion in Latin America. Berkeley: University
    of California Press, 1962. (Paperback.)

Viner, Jacob. Studies in the Theory of Internation-
    al Trade. New York: Harper & Brothers, 1937.

_____. The Customs Union Issue. New York:
    Carnegie Endowment for International Peace,
    1950.

Whitaker, Arthur P. The Western Hemisphere Idea:
    Its Rise and Decline. Ithaca, N.Y.: Cornell
    University Press, 1954.

Wilcox, Clair. A Charter for World Trade. New
    York: The Macmillan Company, 1949.

Williams, Benjamin H. Economic Foreign Policy of
    the United States. New York: McGraw-Hill Book
    Co., 1929.

Articles in Periodicals or Collections

Allen, Robert Loring. "Integration in Less De-
    veloped Countries," Kyklos. Basel, 1961.

Balassa, Bela. "European Integration: Problems and
    Issues," American Economic Review, LIII, No. 2
    (May, 1963) , pp. 175-84.

_____. "Tariff Protection in Industrial Coun-
    tries: An Evaluation," The Journal of Politi-
    cal Economy, LXXIII, No. 6 (December, 1965),
    pp. 573-94.

Barber, Clarence L. "Canadian Tariff Policy,"
    Canadian Journal of Economics and Political
    Science, XXI, No. 4 (November, 1955), pp. 513-
    30.

Catudal, Honoré Marcel. "The Most-Favored-
    Nation Clause and the Courts," American
    Journal of International Law, XXXV, No. 1
    (January, 1941), pp. 41-54.

Cooper, C. A., and B. F. Massell. "Toward a Gen-
    eral Theory of Customs Unions for Developing
    Countries," The Journal of Political Economy,
    LXXIII, No. 5 (October, 1965), pp. 461-76.

Corden, W. M. "The Tariff," The Economics of
    Australian Industry, Alex Hunter, editor.
    Melbourne: Melbourne University Press, 1963.

Culbertson, William S. "Most-Favored-Nation Treat-
    ment," Proceedings of the thirty-first annual
    meeting of the American Society of Inter-
    national Law. Washington, D.C., April 29-
    May 1, 1937.

Decraene, Philippe. "France's Changing Policy in
    Africa," The Reporter (January 13, 1966),
    pp. 37-39.

Deutsch, K. W., and A. Eckstein. "National Indus-
    trialization and the Declining Share of the
    International Economic Sector, 1890-1959,"
    World Politics, No. 13 (1961), pp. 267-99.

Frank, Isaiah. "Issues Before the U. N. Confer-
    ence," Foreign Affairs, XLII, No. 2 (January,
    1964), pp. 210-26.

Green, R. W. "Commonwealth Preference: Tariff
    Duties and Preferences on United Kingdom Ex-
    ports to the Preference Area," <u>Board of Trade</u>
    <u>Journal</u>, CLXXXVIII, No. 3560 (June 11, 1965).

Harberger, Arnold C. "Some Evidence on the Inter-
    national Price Mechanism," <u>The Journal of</u>
    <u>Political Economy</u>, LXV, No. 6 (December, 1957),
    pp. 506-21.

Hornbeck, Stanley Kuhl. "The Most-Favored-Nation
    Clause in Commercial Treaties," <u>Bulletin</u> of the
    University of Wisconsin, No. 343 (January,
    1910), pp. 327-447.

Johnson, Harry G. "An Economic Theory of Protec-
    tionism, Tariff Bargaining, and the Formation
    of Customs Unions," <u>The Journal of Political</u>
    <u>Economy</u>, LXXIII, No. 3 (June, 1965), pp. 256-83.

Krause, Lawrence B. "United States Imports and the
    Tariff," <u>American Economic Review</u>, XLIX, No. 2
    (May, 1959), 542-51.

Kuznets, Simon. "Quantitative Aspects of the Eco-
    nomic Growth of Nations: IX. Level and Struc-
    ture of Foreign Trade: Comparisons for Recent
    Years," <u>Economic Development and Cultural</u>
    <u>Change</u>, XIII, No. 1 (October, 1964).

Lamfalussy, Alexander. "Europe's Progress: Due
    to Common Market?" <u>Lloyds Bank Review</u>
    (October, 1961), pp. 1-16.

Lipsey, Richard G. "Trade Diversion and Welfare,"
    <u>Economica</u>, XXIV (February, 1957), pp. 40-46.

_____. "The Theory of Customs Unions: A General
    Survey," <u>Economic Journal</u>, LXX (September,
    1960), pp. 496-513.

Lodge, George C. "Revolution in Latin America,"
    <u>Foreign Affairs</u>, XLIV, No. 2 (January, 1966),
    pp. 173-97.

Macario, Santiago. "Protectionism and Industriali-
    zation in Latin America," Economic Bulletin for
    Latin America, IX, No. 1 (March, 1964), pp. 61-102.

Mikesell, Raymond F. "The Movement Towards Regional
    Trading Groups in Latin America," Latin American
    Issues, Essays and Comments. New York: Twen-
    tieth Century Fund, 1961, pp. 125-51.

Myint, Hla. "Economic Theory and Underdeveloped
    Countries," The Journal of Political Economy,
    LXXIII, No. 5 (October, 1965), pp. 477-91.

Patterson, Gardner. "Would Tariff Preferences Help
    Economic Development?" Lloyds Bank Review, No.
    76 (April, 1965), pp. 18-30.

Prebisch, Raúl. "Commercial Policy in the Under-
    developed Countries," American Economic Review,
    XLIX (May, 1959), pp. 251-73.

Rom, M. "Customs Unions and Third Countries in
    GATT," Journal of Economic Abstracts, II, No.
    4 (October, 1964), pp. 243-60.

Setser, Vernon. "Did Americans Originate the Condi-
    tional Most-Favored-Nation Clause?" The Journal
    of Modern History, V, No. 3 (September, 1933),
    pp. 319-23.

Taussig, Frank William. "Reciprocity," Quarterly
    Journal of Economics (October, 1892). Reprinted
    in Free Trade and Tariff Reciprocity. New York:
    The Macmillan Company, 1920, pp. 120-33.

Viner, Jacob. "The Most-Favored-Nation Clause in
    American Commercial Treaties," The Journal of
    Political Economy, XXXII, No. 1 (February,
    1924), pp. 101-29.

Visser, L. E. "La clause de la nation la plus
    favorisée dans les traités de commerce," Revue
    de Droit International, IV (1902).

Weintraub, Sidney. "After the U. N. Trade Confer-
    ence: Lessons and Portents," Foreign Affairs,
    XLIII, No. 1 (October, 1964), pp. 37-50.

Williamson, Jeffrey G. "Regional Inequality and
    the Process of National Development: A De-
    scription of the Patterns," Economic Develop-
    ment and Cultural Change, XIII, No 4, Part II
    (July, 1965).

Woods, George D. "The Development Decade in the
    Balance," Foreign Affairs, XLIV, No. 2
    (January, 1966), pp. 206-15.

        Publications of Governments, International
    and Other Organizations, and Learned Societies

Asociacion Latinoamericana de Libre Comercio. "Lista
    de ventajas no extensivas otorgadas a Paraguay
    (Articulo 32, inc. a), 1965." Montevideo.

Bloch, Henry Simon. The Challenge of the World
    Trade Conference. School of International
    Affairs, Columbia University, 1964-65.

Chase Manhattan Bank. The European Markets, A Guide
    for American Businessmen. New York, January,
    1964.

Committee for Economic Development. Trade Negotia-
    tions for a Better Free World Economy. May,
    1964.

Commonwealth Preference in the United Kingdom.
    Political and Economic Planning, 1961.

Cooper, C. A., and B. F. Massell. "A New Look at
    Customs Union Theory." The RAND Corporation,
    November, 1964.

Corden, W. M. Recent Developments in the Theory of
    International Trade. Special paper in interna-
    tional economics. Princeton University, March,
    1965.

Economic Commission for Asia and the Far East. The Scope for Economic Cooperation in Asia and the Far East. E/CN.11/CAEP.1/L.4, August, 1961.

Economic Commission for Europe. Economic Survey of Europe in 1954. Geneva.

_____. Economic Survey of Europe in 1955. Geneva.

_____. Economic Survey of Europe in 1960. E/ECE/419. Geneva, 1961.

General Agreement on Tariffs and Trade. Basic Instruments and Selected Documents (BISD), Vol. I. Geneva, May, 1952.

_____. Basic Instruments and Selected Documents (BISD), First Supplement. Geneva, March, 1953.

_____. Basic Instruments and Selected Documents (BISD), Third Supplement. Geneva, June, 1955.

_____. Basic Instruments and Selected Documents (BISD), Sixth Supplement. Geneva, March, 1958.

_____. Basic Instruments and Selected Documents (BISD), Thirteenth Supplement. Geneva, July, 1965.

_____. International Trade 1963. Geneva, 1964.

_____. "Survey of Progress in the Reduction and Elimination of Barriers Affecting Products Examined by Committee III," Com. III/119. October 21, 1963.

Haas, Ernest B., and Philippe C. Schmitter. The Politics of Economics in Latin American Regionalism: The Latin American Free Trade Association after Four Years of Operation. Monograph No. 2, 1965-66. The Social Science Foundation and the Graduate School of International Studies, University of Denver.

Haberler, Gottfried. A Survey of International Trade
     Theory. International Finance Section, Prince-
     ton University, 1961.

International Bank for Reconstruction and Develop-
     ment. Study on Supplementary Financial
     Measures. Washington, D.C., December 6, 1965.

Johnson, Harry G. "America in the World Economy--
     the Decade Ahead." Selected paper No. 17.
     Graduate School of Business, University of
     Chicago, July, 1965.

League of Nations. 27th Report of the Economic
     Committee. January, 1929.

_____, Economic Committee. Equality of Treat-
     ment in the Present State of International
     Commercial Relations--The Most-Favoured-Nation
     Clause. Geneva, 1936.

Massell, Benton F. "The Distribution of Gains in a
     Common Market." The RAND Corporation, August,
     1964.

Minutes of the International American Conference.
     Held Washington, D.C., October 2, 1889, to
     April 19, 1890.

New Directions for World Trade. Report of a confer-
     ence organized by the Royal Institute of Inter-
     national Affairs, Bellagio, September 16-24,
     1963.

New Zealand's Trade with Australia. Presented to
     the House of Representatives. Wellington:
     New Zealand, Government Printer, 1965.

Nichols, R. T. The Common Market and European
     Unification. Santa Monica, California: The
     RAND Corporation, December, 1965.

Organization of American States. Final Act of the
     Second Special Inter-American Conference.
     Signed in Rio de Janeiro, Brazil, November 30,
     1965.

Pan American Union. Alliance for Progress.
     Official documents emanating from the special
     meeting of the Inter-American Economic and
     Social Council at Ministerial level, held Punta
     del Este, Uruguay, August 5 to 17, 1961.
     Washington, D.C., 1961.

_____. Charter of the Organization of American
     States. Signed at Ninth International Confer-
     ence of American States, Bogota, March 30-
     May 2, 1948.

Proceedings of the United Nations Conference on
     Trade and Development. 8 vols. Geneva, March
     23-June 16, 1964.

"Report to the President of the Special Committee
     on U. S. Trade Relations with East European
     Countries and the Soviet Union." Washington,
     D.C., April 29, 1965.

Riedl, Richard. Exceptions to the Most-Favored-
     Nation Treatment. Report presented to the
     International Chamber of Commerce. London:
     P. S. King & Son, Ltd., 1931.

Staff Papers. Presented to the Commission on
     Foreign Economic Policy, February, 1954. Wash-
     ington, D.C.: Government Printing Office.

"Trade and Development Conference," Issues Before the
     Nineteenth General Assembly. International
     Conciliation, No. 550, Carnegie Endowment for
     International Peace. New York, November, 1964.

Treaties, Conventions, International Acts, Protocols
     and Agreements between the U. S. A. and Other
     Powers, 1776-1909, Vol. I.

Treaty establishing the European Economic Community,
     and connected documents, published by the
     Secretariat of the Interim Committee for the
     Common Market and Euratom, Brussels.

Triffin, Robert. "Notes on Trade Liberalization and
     Regionalism." Material collected by the staff
     for the Subcommittee on Foreign Trade Policy
     of the Committee on Ways and Means, House of
     Representatives, U.S. Congress, 1957, pp.
     483-89.

United Nations. The Growth of World Industry, 1938-
     1961. New York, 1963.

_____. Towards a New Trade Policy for Develop-
     ment. Report by the Secretary-General of the
     United Nations Conference on Trade and Develop-
     ment. New York, 1964.

United Nations Conference on Trade and Development.
     Latin America and the United Nations Conference
     on Trade and Development. Prepared for UNCTAD
     by the ECLA secretariat, E/CONF.46/71, Feb-
     ruary 27, 1964.

_____. Final Act, with Related Documents.
     Geneva, March 23-June 16, 1964. London: Her
     Majesty's Stationery Office, July, 1964. Cmnd.
     2417.

_____. Memorandum Concerning Certain Items on
     the Agenda of the United Nations Conference
     on Trade and Development. Submitted by France,
     E/CONF.46/74, February 27, 1964, and Corr. 1,
     March 30, 1964.

_____. The Alta Gracia Charter. E/CONF.46/100,
     April 10, 1964.

_____. Preferences: Review of Discussions.
     Report by the Secretary-General of the Confer-
     ence, TD/B/AC.1/1 and Corr. 1, March 23, 1965.

_____. Proposals for the Creation of the Latin
     American Common Market. TD/B/11, April 15,
     1965.

_____. Report of the Special Committee on Prefer-
ences. TD/B/C.2/1 and TD/B/AC.1/4, June 4,
1965, and Add.1 to each, June 8, 1965.

_____, and its Preparatory Committee. "Summary
Records."

United Nations, Department of Economic and Social
Affairs. World Economic Survey, 1963. New
York, 1964.

United Nations, Economic and Social Council. World
Economic Trends. E/4059, June 29, 1965.

_____. World Economic Survey, 1964. New York,
1965.

United Nations General Assembly, Twentieth Session.
Activities in the Field of Industrial Develop-
ment. Report of the Second Committee, A/6191,
December 18, 1965.

United States. "An Act to Amend the Tariff Act of
1930," Statutes at Large, XLVIII (March, 1933-
June, 1934), Part 1.

United States Agency for International Development.
Loan Terms, Debt Burden and Development.
Washington, D.C., April, 1965.

United States Chamber of Commerce. Most-Favored-
Nation Treatment and Bargaining Tariffs. Com-
mittee Report, Foreign Commerce Department.
Washington, D.C., March, 1933.

United States Congress, House of Representatives,
Committee on Ways and Means. "Material Prepared by Executive Branch Concerning H.R. 6960,
Automotive Products Trade Act of 1965," April,
1965.

United States Congress, Joint Economic Committee.
Latin American Development and Western Hemisphere Trade. Hearings before the Subcommittee
on Inter-American Relations, September 8-10,

1965. Washington, D.C.: Government Printing
Office, 1965.

_____. The Trade Expansion Act of 1962. Public
Law 87-794, 87th Congress, H.R. 11970, October
11, 1963.

United States Congress, Senate, Committee on Finance.
Philippine Trade Act of 1946 (H.R. 5856). Hearings, 79th Congress, 2d Session, April 2-6, 1946.

United States Department of State. Foreign Relations
of the United States, 1899. Washington, D.C.

_____. Foreign Relations of the United States,
1923. Washington, D.C.

_____. "Havana Charter for an International Trade
Organization." Publication 3206. September,
1948.

United States Tariff Commission. Reciprocity and
Commercial Treaties. Washington, D.C.: Government Printing Office, 1919.

_____. Tariff Bargaining Under Most-Favored-
Nation Treaties. Washington, D.C.: Government
Printing Office, 1933.

Weintraub, Sidney. The Foreign-Exchange Gap of the
Developing Countries. Essays in International
Finance. Princeton University, September, 1965.

Speeches

Ball, George W., Under Secretary of State. Speech
before the United Nations Conference on Trade
and Development, Geneva, March 25, 1964. Department of State press release No. 133, March
25, 1964.

_____. "The Open System in North-South Relations."
Speech before the North Carolina University Symposium, Chapel Hill, April 9, 1964. Department
of State press release No. 156, April 9, 1964.

Brasseur, Maurice, Belgium, Minister for External
    Trade and Technical Assistance, May 17, 1963.
    Statement at Ministerial Meeting of the Con-
    tracting Parties to the General Agreement on
    Tariffs and Trade. Press release GATT/750.

Dillon, Douglas, Under Secretary of State. Depart-
    ment of State Bulletin, March 21, 1960.

Eisenhower, Dwight D., March 8, 1960. Report to the
    nation by the President of the U.S. Depart-
    ment of State Bulletin, March 28, 1960.

Garrido Torres, José, of Brazil. Speech before
    plenary session of the United Nations Economic
    Commission for Latin America, Mexico City,
    May 11, 1965. ECLA Documento informativo
    No. 41.

Johnson, Lyndon B. Remarks by President Johnson at
    Howard University, June 4, 1965. White House
    press release.

Kennedy, John F. Remarks by the President of the
    U.S. on the Alliance for Progress, March 13,
    1961. Department of State Bulletin, April 13,
    1961.

McEwen, J., Deputy Prime Minister and Minister for
    Trade and Industry of Australia. Statement in
    the Australian House of Representatives, May
    19, 1965.

Prebisch, Raul. Speech at Viña del Mar, Chile,
    March 22, 1965. Unofficial translation from
    Spanish by United States Embassy, Santiago,
    Chile, Airgram A-894 of April 9, 1965.

_____. Speech before plenary session of the
    United Nations Economic Commission for Latin
    America, Mexico City, May 8, 1965. ECLA
    Documento informativo No. 11.

Rostow, W. W., Counselor and Chairman of the Policy
    Planning Council, Department of State. "Eco-
    nomic Development: Some Lessons of a Common
    Experience." Address before the American
    Chamber of Commerce, Mexico City, August 19,
    1963. Department of State press release No. 431.
    August 19, 1963.

_____. "How to Make a National Market." Address
    at the Farm Equipment Institute, New Orleans,
    October 1, 1963.

_____. "Some Lessons of Economic Development
    Since the War." Address before the Institute
    of Economic Development, Madrid, October 7,
    1964. Department of State press release No.
    438, October 7, 1964.

_____. "Economic Development in Asia." Address
    in Tokyo, April 23, 1965. Department of State
    press release No. 80, April 22, 1965.

_____. "Present Status of International Develop-
    ment Policy." Address before Society for
    International Development, Washington, D.C.,
    June 2, 1965.

_____. "The Concept of a National Market and its
    Economic Growth Implications." Speech before
    American Marketing Association, September 1,
    1965. Department of State press release No.
    202, August 31, 1965.

Rubottom, R. R., Jr., Assistant Secretary of State
    for Inter-American Affairs, April 9, 1960.
    Department of State Bulletin, May 2, 1960.

Washington, George. Farewell Address, September 17,
    1796. In James D. Richardson, A Compilation
    of the Messages and Papers of the Presidents,
    1789-1897. Washington, D.C.: Government
    Printing Office, 1896.

Wilson, Woodrow. Address by the President to a
      Joint Session of the Two Houses of the Congress,
      January 18, 1918. Foreign Relations of the
      United States, 1918. Supplement 1: The World
      War, Vol. I.

Newspapers and Magazines

Business Week, "Outlook" column, January 23, 1964.

The Economist, London. "An Economic Survey of Latin
      America," special section on September 25, 1965.

Journal of Commerce, December 2, 1965.

Lippmann, Walter, columns in the Washington Post,
      December 14 and 16, 1965.

The New York Times, August 1, 1965; November 27,
      1965; December 17, 1965.

Washington Post, January 17, 1965; September 22 and
      30, 1965; October 4, 1965.

Unpublished Materials

Strauss, Frederick. "Report on the United Nations
      Conference on Trade and Development." Unpub-
      lished report by U.S. Department of Commerce
      participant at the Conference, dated July,
      1964.

United States Department of State. "American Com-
      mercial Policy, with Particular Reference to
      the Most-Favored-Nation Clause (1620-1923)."
      Unpublished research project No. 725, Histor-
      ical Studies Division, Historical Office,
      Bureau of Public Affairs, August, 1965.

_____, Economic Adviser. Memorandum to the Sec-
      retary of State, March 12, 1924.

_____, Office of the Foreign Trade Adviser.
    "Commercial Policy," Memorandum to the Secre-
    tary of State, May 23, 1922.

Vanek, Jaroslav. "Discriminatory Liberalization of
    Imports of Manufactures from the LDC's by Ad-
    vanced Countries." Unpublished comment, undated,
    but written in 1964.

ABOUT THE AUTHOR

Sidney Weintraub, a career foreign service officer, has lived and worked in developing countries in Africa, Asia, and Latin America. He is now the Counselor for Economic Affairs of the American Embassy in Santiago, Chile, and simultaneously the Deputy Director of the U.S. AID Mission to Chile.

Until mid-1965, Mr. Weintraub was the Department of State's chief of commercial policy. In that capacity he attended all three preparatory meetings leading up to the first United Nations Conference on Trade and Development in 1964, UNCTAD itself, and various post-UNCTAD meetings which dealt with UNCTAD resolutions. He played an important role in the formulation of United States trade policy, not only in connection with UNCTAD, but in other contexts as well, such as for the Kennedy round of trade negotiations. Mr. Weintraub is not now a commercial policy-maker for the United States Government, and this study represents his personal views and not official policy.

He has participated in meetings of the United Nations in New York and Geneva, the General Agreement on Tariffs and Trade in Geneva, the Organization for Economic Cooperation and Development in Paris, the Economic Commission for Latin America in Santiago, the Inter-American Economic and Social Council in Lima and Sao Paulo and Washington, and the Economic Commission for Asia and the Far East in Bangkok, among others.

Mr. Weintraub received a Ph. D. degree in economics from The American University in Washington, D.C. He is the author of The Foreign-Exchange Gap of the Developing Countries (Princeton, N. J.: Princeton University Press, 1965), "After the UN Trade Conference: Lessons and Portents" (Foreign Affairs, October, 1964), and other publications.